here. now.

here.

now.

a catholic guide to the good life

Our Sunday Visitor Publishing Division
Our Sunday Visitor, Inc.
Huntington, Indiana 46750

AMY WELBORN

To Christopher, David, Katie, Joseph, and Michael

Contents

Out of the Tombs

Forget everything you thought you knew about Jesus.

Now, listen.

It's a bright clear day in Galilee, and this man — this friendly, intense and, in ways, mysterious Jesus — gets off a boat in a place called Gerasene, right on the lake.

As usual, he's got his friends with him, friends who sometimes get him, but more often don't. They stick with him anyway, because this whole thing seems to be about something other than achieving untouchable intellectual precision and understanding. Something.

The group comes ashore, and a man meets them. The man is crazy, they say. Or worse, possessed. So deeply taken up by evil, death and pain that he lives in the most appropriate place: among the tombs. With the dead, because he might as well be.

Jesus takes a look. Asks a question.

"What is your name?"

"Legion!" is the answer.

Many. An army of evil, killing the soul, draining it of life and hope.

And Jesus drives the demons out — into a herd of pigs. They run off a cliff.

They're gone, those demons. The man is free. He puts his clothes on, he's at peace, he's ready to live again, to climb out of the tombs, his prison and his chains. He meets his fellow villagers.

They are petrified.

The villagers, the witnesses to this transformation, turn to Jesus and beg him — to help them?

No.

They beg him to get out. Leave, they say. Go back across the lake. Please.

So he does, but only after taking the formerly dead, now fully alive man, eyes wide open, aside and telling him, "You go, too. Leave these tombs and go back home. Go tell what God has done for you. Do it now." (Mk 5:1-20)

What's wrong with these people? They saw death turn to life, evil to joy and promise, and they respond — with fear? They beg the one who brought that life, who drew this poor guy out of the tombs into the sunlight and freedom, to leave them?

Given the choice between pain and joy, they choose . . . pain? Why?

Why. Good question. Great question.

Why do we do this? Because, you know, we do — all the time. We say we want to be happy and at peace, we really, really do . . . but when the hand reaches out to us . . . we turn away, close the door, and tell him to go back across the lake. Please.

This book is about Jesus. It's also about the man living in the tombs, the villagers, and us.

You want to be happy, and so do I. Is it possible? Or, more importantly, is it possible to find a happiness that lasts, that we can't lose?

Is it possible to climb out of the tombs and stay out?

Jesus, obviously, says yes.

Why are we so afraid of that yes?

A lot of the time we think of our relationship with God as something that's just about the future. We'll be more serious about it when we're a bit older, or when we're settled in careers, or married and have kids. In the future.

We'll have plenty of time, we say.

Time for what?

Time to waste, time to take wrong turns, time to be disappointed, used up and thrown away by the world, again and again and again? Time to scramble after the approval of other human beings, submit to the pressures they place on us, and time to feel awful about ourselves when we don't meet their standards? Time to explore the geography of that graveyard, to memorize the position of each stone, as we wander from this crushed hope to that shattered ideal to this broken promise?

Please notice that Jesus didn't tell the possessed man to wait. He lifted him up, healed him, and brought him back to life right there and then.

That's real life. For you, right here, right now.

If you dare.

SECTION I

Here. Now.

CHAPTER 1

Center, Found

"Just let me be myself. Please."

It's what so many of us want from the world. The simple free-dom to be ourselves. With one condition, of course:

"As long as no one thinks I'm lame."

That seems to be how it works, all the time, from all time. My oldest son, now in his early 20s, once observed that he and his friends, in their quest for radical individuality, ended up all dress-ing in the same style, playing the same music, and talking in iden-tical slang and code words. Funny how that happens.

We all want to be ourselves, but sometimes we operate under a curious misunderstanding of what that means. We think that the "myself" we're trying to be is some totally independent being, free from any outside influences. That's just not the way it is, though.

No one creates themselves from scratch. Well, no one creates *themselves* at all, of course, but even when it comes to style, val-ues, career direction, expectations, and even likes and dislikes, we are the product of an interaction with other forces and voices out-side ourselves.

Thinking . . .

... Does your physical appearance matter to you? Why? Who told you it should matter?

...What kind of music do you like? Why? How did that type of music come into your life?

... What are your career goals? Why? Where did the standards that you're using to judge how successful you are come from?

... When you imagine a happy life, now and in the future, what do you think of? Be honest. Where does your understanding of "happiness" come from?

Well? What did you come up with? Are you completely in charge of your own life, the Master or Mistress of your own Universe, totally beyond the influence of others?

Didn't think so. None of us is.

It's not that we're slaves of fate, either — robots acting only in response to stimuli and commands. Who you are is the result of an interaction, a dynamic between your free will, your uniqueness, the choices that your world presents, and what it's taught you is valuable and important.

But if you answered those questions in the box honestly, you might have confronted that Myth of Total Independence. In a rather shockingly major way, your life is a response to voices and challenges raised by others. Nothing is excluded, not how you style your hair, not how you define what "happiness" means for you.

Listening . . .

... What messages did you pick up from your family about your value? Do you find yourself trying to please or argue against those messages in your choices?

... What messages do your peers give you about what makes you valuable?

... What messages does your culture — your music, mass media — give you about what makes your life worth living? Do you believe them?

Forgetting someone?

You may have noticed that in all of this talk about voices, forces and influences, we seem to have left someone out.

Ah, yes. God.

You're reading this book, so it's probably safe to assume that you're a baptized Christian — maybe even a baptized and confirmed Catholic who goes to Mass regularly. Or at least a lot, relatively speaking.

So tell me. Where's God in your life?

And I don't mean that in terms in vague, abstract terms. I mean . . . really. As you live your life, make your decisions, open your mouth to speak, spend your money, choose your career and pursue it . . . where's God?

I'll leave that up to you to figure out and confront. But after you've thought about it a bit, come back here and confront this:

If you say you're a Christian, you're saying that God is at the center of your life.

Because, you see, that's what being a Christian is. It's not a club dreamed up to keep you busy or make you feel like a useful member of society. It's not about just having a religious label because a religious label is a useful thing to have in our society. Believe it or not, it's not even about having standards or guidelines to live by or being a better person.

It's about this question:

Who do you belong to?

And this one:

Who's your judge?

Oh, and this one, too:

Who loves you, without end or limit?

In other words, being Christian — contrary to what you might have heard — is most definitely not about obligations, rules, standards, or membership. Oh, those things may spin out of our Christian identity, especially as we live it in the world with others, but the heart of it all goes a whole lot deeper than that.

It's about who's in charge, who you listen to and, to be honest, who's got your best interest at heart.

As we've seen already, there's no lack of voices competing for your ear, no lack of authorities demanding your allegiance, and no lack of amusements promising pleasure.

In other words, everyone is promising to save you.

Everyone is promising to lead you on roads that will bring you to happiness, joy, and satisfaction.

(Often at a price. You might want to think about that, as well.)

Bottom line: If you're a Christian, you believe none of them.

Second-to-the-bottom line: They can't do what they promise anyway, so why bother?

> "But God said to him, 'Fool! This night your soul is required of you; and the things you have prepared, whose will they be?' So is he who lays up treasure for himself, and is not rich toward God."
>
> Lk 12:20, 21

Here's what it all comes down to: So many of us — perhaps even most of us — are deep in the rut of thinking about "religion" and "faith" as something we "have to do." We may have internalized the importance of "putting God first" in our lives, but I'd bet that for most of us, even that has the vaguest aroma of threat around it: "Put God first . . . or else!"

But if you get beyond what you think you know and even what some well-meaning teachers along the way may have said — if you actually look into the roots of your faith: the Scriptures, the prayers and traditions of Catholicism — what you find is that this call to put God first, a call that's sent out to you at your baptism, again at your confirmation, and over and over in between, is not at all about threats or obligations.

It's about love.

Just work through this with me. It will only take a minute.

Who made you?

God, you say. Fantastic. Now — do you really believe that? Do you believe that you were thought up by God, formed by God and brought to life by God?

Yes? Now consider this . . . why would God do that?

Maybe . . . because he *wants* you to be here. Maybe . . . *because He loves you.* Maybe . . . *God loves you so much he wants you to exist.*

Next question.

Given that rather amazing fact, who knows you the best, wants the best for you, and desires your happiness the most?

Got it. Even more than your parents do, even more than your significant other or your best friend . . . *even more than you yourself* . . .

God knows you the most intimately, loves you the most, and most deeply wants your happiness. Now and even beyond that.

So, sit down and consider the cacophony that surrounds you, all that noise rattling in your head. If you want happiness, if you want the good life, if you want it here and now . . .

Who are you going to listen to?

Who's got the answer to when you're wondering what's best for you to do with either this moment in time or your life in general?

Who has nothing personal at stake — no parental pride, no profit motive, no security — in your response?

And whose happiness will stay steady, not rot, not be stolen, not fade with time or go out of style in two years, never backfire, and not even care if you're young and productive or old and helpless?

Who?

It's called . . .

Faith.

Believe it or not, that's what I've been talking about this whole time.

This trust that God created you, God loves you, and God is, in the end, the only one to whom you're accountable, the only voice worth listening to?

That's exactly what faith is.

All of those "great people of faith" that you've spent your life hearing about aren't considered holy or saints because they handed their lives over to an institution, a set of rules, or whatever their parents taught them.

No, they did something different, something that might fall outside your assumptions of what religion is all about. They handed their lives over to God. Not out of fear or habit, but because they understood this:

If God is God, then who else is worth listening to?

Faith in God is just that . . . faith that God created you, every person on earth, and besides that, the universe. God did this thing out of love, which means that we're not here as pieces in a game, subjects in an experiment, or parts of a machine. We're here as children God created, loves, wants the best for and, most important of all, knows the best for. Even you. Here. Now.

That's faith.

Is it yours?

CHAPTER 2

The Search Is On

God is God, all right.

But where to find Him?

A pressing, important question. One that we too often answer in ways that take us in wrong directions and waste a lot of time.

Let's try not to do that so much anymore. Shall we?

Journeys and searches

It's one thing to know, logically, that we should be listening to God, but it's a completely different thing to actually live it.

Well, here's where that new mindset I've been talking about — seeing religion and spirituality as gifts instead of obligations — really comes in handy. Wrap your brain around this:

If God did create you, if God is moving in your heart and inviting you to live the good life, wouldn't it be unspeakably cruel if this same God made the question of figuring out what He's saying an unsolvable mystery? If God put these yearnings and hopes in your heart, and then kept the path to fulfilling them hidden under a tarp or buried in the ground?

Yes, it would be cruel. Nonsensical and weird, besides.

So there you have the second step in faith. The first was believing in and making a decision to live in the reality of God's love for you (and everyone else, too, remember. Sometimes we forget that angle. Makes a difference.). The second is believing that the conversation isn't one-sided. It's not just you asking, wondering, and searching. God's talking. God's reaching out. God's handing you a cool drink of water, serving up a banquet, inviting you out of the tombs, and even giving you a push in the right direction sometimes.

The answer is….

I'll be totally honest with you right now and tell you that for me, it begins and ends with Jesus. Without Jesus, the mystery of God really is murky, dark, abstract, and even a little frightening, as we contemplate the countless "concepts of God" and "ways to the divine" that have been dreamed up over the centuries and that people still latch onto today.

But with Jesus, things are clearer.

I'm going to do what might seem like a strange thing and work backward here. I'm going to start with the end of the Jesus story, not the beginning. But maybe it is the beginning after all. Confused yet?

In the fourth decade of what we call the first century, something happened. A bunch of uneducated, mostly illiterate lower-class Jewish guys from a backwater of the Roman Empire started talking about something exceedingly odd. Their teacher and friend Jesus, who had been executed by the Roman authorities, had risen from the dead. It wasn't just this really unusual event they focused on, though — they were intent on talking about the *meaning* of this event, as well.

And what did it mean? What did they say about it?

This Jesus God raised up, and of that we all are witnesses.

Being therefore exalted at the right hand of God, and having received from the Father the promise of the Holy Spirit, he has poured out this which you see and hear. . . .

> ...God has made him both Lord and Christ...
>
> ...Repent, and be baptized every one of you in the name of Jesus Christ for the forgiveness of your sins; and you shall receive the gift of the Holy Spirit...
>
> Acts 2:32, 33, 36, 38

In other words, Peter was saying, God's power is poured out through Jesus, a power that can heal sinful hearts and bring us into intimacy with God — and since God is love, God is truth, and God is eternal life — that means into intimacy with all of that stuff. *Love, truth, and life, into our hearts and lives, here, now.*

This is what these uneducated, previously completely anonymous guys did. They went out and started talking up a storm and wouldn't stop, no matter what the threat, and there were many. Most of these original guys were martyred because they *wouldn't* stop talking.

So it's reasonable to think that they might have been telling the truth.

Isn't it?

People don't generally submit to the sword for what they know is a lie. Would you? It's not as if these guys were gaining power, influence or wealth from what they were saying. It's not as if their lives weren't completely disrupted or anything, right? What other motive for doing this could there be other than... *it was true. It happened. They couldn't help but share what they called "good news."*

So now, keep walking with me. The apostles told the truth about what had happened to Jesus and what had happened to them. That means (obviously) that what they said about Jesus was ... *true.* It means that what a few decades later was recorded as their memories of Jesus and the stories they told, in what we call the Gospels, is... *true. It happened.*

And what the Gospels testify to is this: that through Jesus, we know God. Through Jesus, we know how much God loves us. Through Jesus, we can see what God does in the world. Through Jesus . . . we can hear, talk to, and touch God.

> That which was from the beginning, which we have heard, which we have seen with our eyes, which we have looked upon and touched with our hands, concerning the word of life—the life was made manifest, and we saw it, and testify to it, and proclaim to you the eternal life which was with the Father and was made manifest to us —that which we have seen and heard we proclaim also to you, so that you may have fellowship with us; and our fellowship is with the Father and with his Son Jesus Christ. And we are writing this that our joy may be complete.
>
> 1 Jn 1:1-4

There are lots of ways to talk about religion, and one of the more popular angles these days is to get all ethereal and talk about "stories." There are, it's said, lots of "stories" out there that express truths about life and eternity. Your job, as a spiritually curious person, is to find the "story" that fits you best. What resonates with you? What is most meaningful to you? Find something? Fantastic! Now live by it . . . but remember, it's just your story that you're going to live by. Your truth. It's not necessarily true for me or for anyone else.

But if it's true and meaningful to you? Love it. Live in that story.

Until you get bored.

Then maybe it's time to find another story, right?

I don't know about you, but this really common way of talking about spirituality bores me. I am just not into spending my already short time on earth jumping between this story and that myth to give me a reason to get up in the morning and do some good.

Frankly, if it's not true—I mean, really and truly true—it's not worth getting up Sunday morning for, much less giving my life to.

I don't accept that kind of thing in relationships with other human beings — saying, "Well, tell me a good story that I'm comfortable with, and I'll spend the rest of my life with you." No. What I want is love and presence and commitment. I want to give it, and I want to live it — not a "story."

And I'll tell you something else. When you look at two thousand years of Christian tradition — or whatever bits of it you're familiar with — and you consider the people we call saints, you don't find men and women blathering on about meaningful stories and many paths to inner peace.

No, you find men and women living in relationship to a *person.* That person is, of course, Jesus, whose path they follow, to whom they speak every day, who strengthens them and forgives them. They didn't give their lives to bringing love and life to the most impoverished (which is what most saints seem to spend their lives doing, oddly enough) because a "story" they found meaningful inspired them to do so. No. They reached out because their dearest friend, companion, and brother Jesus had told them, "When you help them, you help me," had told them that when they die to self they would live, and they had found every word to be absolutely true.

Because, in getting into that relationship with that real Jesus, that true Jesus, they had found life and joy. Read the stuff they've written. Read about them. These saints —they're happy people. Even in the midst of suffering, they found joy. Every one of them could read that story of the man being brought out of the tombs and nod in recognition. *Yes. Been there. Done that. Been . . . saved.*

The joy they describe? As much joy as you've found in the midst of the material comfort and physical pleasure of your own life.

Probably even more.

Here. Now.

Bottom line

If you love someone — friend, significant other, spouse — what are you going to give him or her? What are you going to say about you, that person, and your life?

Are you going to say, "Know in general that I care about you, but don't come any closer"?

Or maybe, "Call me friend, but beyond that, find a story or make up a myth about me that makes sense to you, and base our life together on that"?

I doubt it. You wouldn't do that because that's just not love. Love is really giving of your real self, of knowing and being known ... of *presence*. And if you wouldn't do it, I sincerely doubt God would either.

And that's the bottom line. God made you because He loves you. After He made you, He didn't abandon you to fate, the whims of life or whatever story your imagination can dream up and whatever your emotions find meaningful today (but maybe not tomorrow).

He's with you — in a lot of ways, that's true — but most spectacularly, in this absolutely sure, certain way called Jesus, a real person whom other real people have been dying for you to know. Literally.

This faith business — this religion stuff — in the end, no matter what you might think, no matter how poorly it may have been presented to you by your teachers and other elders ... *is not about rules, threats or obligations.*

At the core of the Christian faith is nothing more than a gift.

It's the gift of the God who loved you into existence and is *just not going to leave you without answers.*

Get it?

God made you. Made you to be joyful. If you believe that, then you've got to know that the way to that joy comes from the one who knows best, the one who made you, that being God.

Who has not only given you the gift of life, but the gift of knowing Him throughout that precious life, and knowing how to live it joyfully.

The gift has a name.

Jesus.

Are you relieved? I am. Makes me want to know more, too. Makes me want to say thanks, because if there's anything we can agree on, it's that it's a mess out there, and it's hard to know whom to trust.

But now, looking up from our home in the tombs . . . we know.

CHAPTER 3

More Good News

Life: God-given.

Happiness: God's aware of the issue. On top of it, even.

The way there: since God is God . . . listen.

To whom: Jesus. Not because there's a rule (because there isn't), but because it just makes sense.

Got it. No codes, no secret handshakes, no insurmountable mountains, no dangling on a string.

But . . . where?

In black and white . . . really

A really common answer to that question is, "In my heart." All I have to do is just listen to what God is telling me . . . in my heart.

Sounds great, and it's even true. But with a twist.

Because you know how hearts are. You know how voices in your head are. You've probably spent some time wondering, "Is what I'm sensing I should do really from God? Or is it just my wishful thinking, or my habits, or maybe even my parents' voices?" Or, we should add, my knee-jerk reaction *against* my parents' voices?

The truth is, a lot of people—yours truly included—have done a lot of mediocre or even bad things because we just went with what we decided God was telling us "in our hearts," only to admit, years later, that we might have been listening to something in our hearts, but it probably wasn't God . . . because God certainly wouldn't have wanted us to hurt another person that way, or waste our time in that way.

So, even if we've decided that listening to God's voice above all others is what we want to do . . . how do we know?

Again, not as much a mystery as it seems. Because you know, if it were a deep, unanswerable puzzle with no sure solution, we'd be back to the God who's no more than a trickster, ready to laugh at our bumblings down here and play hide-and-go-seek with us. No God of Love is that one.

> Think this one through:
>
> How do you know your friends or a boyfriend/girlfriend cares about you?
>
> Just because they say it? Is that why you believe them?
>
> Or do you have evidence and experience to help you understand the truth of their words?
>
> * You've experienced their care in concrete ways
>
> * You're living out of a certain definition of "love," "care," and "friendship"

In other words, you know your friends care because you have their past behavior to compare their words to, and you also can define those words.

Same with God. Same with the gift of Jesus and what all of this means for your life and your happiness.

Read the Bible lately?

The source

More specifically, the New Testament, and most specifically of all, the Gospels. Any of them? A book? A chapter? A verse, maybe?

If not, your confusion about what in the world God could be saying to you, what it all means, and what God wants you to do with your life, is perfectly understandable.

Because, you see, if you're not familiar with what Jesus said about life, happiness, and God . . . of course you're going to be really at sea when you try to discern whether the motions of your spirit and heart are from him — or someone else.

It's like trying to figure out if someone you just met, this second, who's claiming to give you some really good investment advice, should be trusted. What do you have to base it on? You don't know them, you don't know what kind of person they are, what they've said before to other people . . . you just don't know.

So, no excuses. Not anymore. If you're serious about this God-leading-me business, you just have to get yourself a Bible, and you have to start reading it, *especially* the Gospels. If you've traveled with me this far, and have been nodding along with the *God made me, God knows what's best* song . . . then it's time.

And once more . . . not because you have to or else. But because it's a gift.

You've got questions. You really, really want to lead the good life. You don't want to wait.

Then why . . . are you waiting?

CHOOSING A BIBLE:

- First, look for a **Catholic** edition of the Bible. Any other edition won't have all of the books that Catholics have always considered part of Scripture.
- Look for a translation with good notes, and maybe some maps as well. Your reading of Scripture should be primarily prayerful and spiritual, but there are a

lot of points in Scripture that need explaining to 21st-century readers.

- Some of the more popular translations for Catholics are:

  * The New American Bible (this is the translation that's used at Mass)

  * The New Jerusalem Bible

  * The Revised Standard Version (RSV) or the New Revised Standard Version (NRSV)

  * These are the best translations; just be sure, again, you pick out the Catholic edition.

  * In addition, there are Bibles with specially designed supplemental material like the *Catholic Answer Bible,* which contains answers to common questions about the Catholic faith, and the *My Daily Catholic Bible,* which divides the Bible into daily reading sections designed to take you through the entire text in a year.

Can I trust it?

I'm not going to take for granted that you're going to answer "yes" to that question. After all, even if you've been educated in Catholic schools, there's a good chance that along the way you've absorbed certain ideas about these Gospels I'm encouraging you to read.

You might have heard that they were composed a few decades after Jesus' death and resurrection (true), and because of that, they're too distant from the original events to give us any accurate information about Jesus (false).

You might have heard that the origins of the Gospels are in oral tradition (true), and because of that, we can't trust them to tell the truth (false).

You might have heard that the Gospel writers were interested in talking about the story of Jesus in a way that would help their own particular audiences understand Jesus (true), and because of that, they're more useful for what they tell us about those audiences than what they tell us about Jesus himself (false).

You might have heard that the Gospels contain differences and discrepancies in certain details (true), and because of that, there's no way to tell what really happened (false).

Now's not the time—and this isn't the place—to give you a complete course on Bible-reading, but I do want to answer those concerns. Because if you start reading the Gospels with all of that in your head . . . you'll find your heart less, not more, open to encountering Jesus there.

Here's the bottom line: The Gospels, all written down thirty to sixty years after Jesus' life, and the other New Testament writings (especially the letters of Paul, the first of which was probably written no more than twenty years after Jesus' life on earth) were all composed before the end of the first century, and—this is important—they *all tell the same story. They all reveal the same Jesus.*

Not to mention that they also *all share essentially the same experience of Jesus*—that those who knew him experienced healing, life, truth, redemption . . . *God's presence.*

> Inasmuch as many have undertaken to compile a narrative of the things which have been accomplished among us, just as they were delivered to us by those who from the beginning were eyewitnesses and ministers of the word, it seemed good to me also, having followed all things closely for some time past, to write an orderly account for you, most excellent Theophilus, that you may know the truth concerning the things of which you have been informed.
>
> Lk 1:1-4

Sure, it's easy to blow off the New Testament if you've never read it, as some of my students used to do. They'd lean back in their seats, filled with sixteen years of wisdom, and ask, "How do we know that someone just didn't make it all up?"

Well, just read them, my friend. What do you find?

You find documents that are almost painfully real. You know, if you're going to make stuff up, you're probably *not* going to insert stories that make the early leaders of your religion — the apostles — look pretty much like bumbling fools throughout the whole story, consistently and really without exception. You're probably *not* going to have the founder of your religion executed in the manner reserved for the most despicable criminals, and you're probably *not* going to have his empty tomb discovered by women, the half of humanity whose word was not even accepted as testimony in court in the ancient world.

You're just not.

And, by the way, most people wouldn't die for things they just made up. Which is exactly what all of these apostles ended up doing.

There are lots and lots of reasons to trust that the Gospels are telling us the truth about Jesus, and not one of those reasons starts with "Because I say so" or "Because you have to."

When you actually sit down and read the New Testament, you find, not just a very real and authentic-sounding story, but also a consistent one, too — one that its writers say is based on the testimony of witnesses:

> This is the disciple who is bearing witness to these things, and who has written these things; and we know that his testimony is true. But there are also many other things which Jesus did; were every one of them to be written, I suppose that the world itself could not contain the books that would be written.
>
> Jn 21:24-25

So, sure, the texts of what we call the Gospels may not have been written down until a few decades after Jesus' life, but that was not unusual in the ancient world at all, nor was the fact that the stories were first preserved orally. This was, as were all ancient cultures, a world that for the most part preserved all of its culture orally, and did so with great care. Most of Homer, the ancient Greek epic poet, was passed down orally long before it was ever written down. The fact is, the means to write things down were at a premium — it just wasn't done on a daily basis.

And, sure, there are discrepancies in some details (not as many as you think, by the way), but absolutely nothing that impacts the basic picture we have of Jesus: He's not preaching God's forgiveness here, and then excluding sinners there. He's not telling his disciples the necessity of suffering in one place and then advising them to avoid it in another. He's not proclaiming the blessedness of the poor in one place and then excusing the wealthy in another. He's not calling Peter to be the head of his disciples in one Gospel and Andrew in another. He's not crucified in one account and stoned to death in another.

The experience of those who knew and encountered Jesus is consistent as well . . . even after his resurrection. All repentant sinners who come to Jesus with an open heart experience forgiveness and amazing freedom. All fearful religious hypocrites are infuriated by him. All are changed and understand, somehow, that through Jesus, they have met God.

Trustworthy

Listen. Here's why you should read the Gospels and trust them to tell you the truth about Jesus:

- There was no logical reason for anyone associated with Jesus to fabricate lies about him. There would have been no benefit.
- The books that we now call the "New Testament" were chosen by ancient Christians with great care. They knew their traditions and history — they knew which books had the deepest ties to the apostles' witness. That witness had been passed down to them — the books they eventually decided to include were those that were most faithful to the Jesus the apostles and others knew and talked about.

No crazy, outlandish stuff, no big, unrealistic heroics, no over-explanations to make everything "fit," and even (when it comes to the apostles) some flaws.

- There's nothing else. I mean it. Lots of people in the past and even in the present have come along with writings "about" Jesus that try to tell you the "real story" or some recently discovered "secret"—but they're all just works of imagination. The writings about Jesus that date closest to his life are the Gospels and the letters of Paul. Period. Why bother with anything else?

So. We go back on that path, one more time. . . .

You want to dig deeper into God's presence in your life? You want to know what He's saying to you here and now, as opposed to what you *think* He might be saying?

You've got to get into Jesus through the Gospels. Got to. Even if it just means listening more carefully when you go to Mass, you've got to do it. Or else you're just back in that swamp, surrounded by mysterious chirps and howls, with mysterious glints of light in the distance, with no way of knowing what's really going to get you out of there, no way of figuring out what light will lead you to the road and which ones will take you more deeply into darkness.

Want to know what God's saying to you about your happiness, about your life, here and now? Listen to your heart, yes indeed, and then compare what you *think* Jesus is saying there to the *sure thing* of what Jesus says about life, sacrifice, forgiveness and suffering in the Gospels.

It's the only way you're going to be able to recognize his voice when he calls . . . the only way you're going to know who's calling you out of the tombs into life.

CHAPTER 4

What He Said

Know Jesus. Talk to him. Listen. Hold up your conscience to what Jesus is all about. He's solid and true and he loves you more than you even love yourself.

(Believe it or not.)

You know it. You've got the book. *The* Book. You're going to start connecting with Jesus, and listening to him. What are you going to hear?

First place

If you want to make sense of Jesus, and are really open to him to help *you* make sense of *you,* first things first.

And for Jesus, first thing is God.

This actually might surprise some of you, who just might have been under the impression that the focus of Jesus' teaching is *Be Nice.*

Sorry. Oh, it's in there, but if *Be Nice* were the essence of what Jesus was about, there would be absolutely nothing to distinguish him from any other religious teacher or philosopher who's ever lived . . . because not a one of them hasn't put *Be Nice* at the center.

There's more to Jesus than that.

(Which also might mean that there's more to following Jesus than that... something to think about.)

No, front and center for Jesus, everything he said to us and everything he did is... God.

Someone asked what the greatest commandment is.

He answered, "You shall love the Lord your God with all your heart, and with all your soul, and with all your mind." (Mt 22:37; it's a reference, of course, to the Jewish Law: Deut 6:5.)

Someone asked him how to pray.

He answered, "Father, hallowed be your name, your kingdom come... "

In other places, Jesus tells us that discipleship means putting, if necessary, even family aside. He tells us that when it comes to life and what we do with it — depend on God like the lilies of the field do, build your house on rock (that would be God) — and everything else will fall into place.

Why this? Why not just *Be Nice?*

Because without God, how do we even know what "Be Nice" means?

You probably see where this is going. We've talked about the limits of "following your heart." We're pretty sure that "be nice" can be twisted this way and that until it essentially means nothing, and can even result, ultimately, in harm.

Those guidelines to behavior, which so many of us have mistakenly adopted as the essence of Christian life, are *nothing* if there are no standards. They're pointless and empty because they're not *about anything.* People can do all kinds of mediocre or even terrible things, assuring you all the while that they're just following their hearts or trying to do what they think is best for you.

With God, we've got Truth to hold up against the yearnings of our hearts or what we suspect might be kindness or goodness — to tell us if we're right.

Or not.

There are a lot of different ways to get to know Jesus through the Gospels. You could pick a Gospel, and read a chapter a night. You could decide to take it all in and get the big picture—read all four Gospels over the course of a month, maybe, and then go back and spend more time (the rest of your life, maybe?) on smaller pieces. Or you could just start by listening really carefully and prayerfully when the Gospel's proclaimed at Mass.

God's world . . . we're only living in it

Jesus has us thinking about God, moving God into the center. But he's also doing something else. He's showing us what life with God is. He's talking and living the Kingdom of God.

It's all over the Gospels, from the very beginning. They're all consistent in characterizing Jesus' preaching as centered on the Kingdom of God.

Which is . . . what?

Simple, but deep. The Kingdom (or reign) of God happens where and when God reigns. It's more than heaven, although that's the fulfillment of God's kingdom, no doubt. No, as Jesus says, the Kingdom of God is here among us, as well (Lk 17:21). As some people like to say, it's an "already, but not yet" kind of situation.

It's a mystery, for sure, and a dynamic one. God rules all of his creation, no doubt. But because human beings are a part of that creation, and God made us with this thing called free will, there's a level at which our choices play a role in the fullness of God's presence.

It's not that our actions bring the fullness of God's reign about. It's pretty ridiculous to think about God's presence being dependent on our attitudes and actions. But the whole thing is a lot like the dynamic of human love. Someone can stand in front of you and mentally, spiritually, and emotionally just pour love out in your direction. Can just stand there and love you to pieces, and let you know it.

But if your heart is closed . . . so what? What happens? Can the love "reign" in your life or even shed a tiny sliver of light? No. If you're not open, it can't.

So, sure, God can do anything he wants. But because He created us with free will, and for some crazy reason gave us a role in bringing His creation to life and fullness, making us partners with Him in a way . . . our response matters.

This Kingdom of God, then, is something Jesus talks about a lot because it really defines what we're all about in this life. Want to be a part of the greatness God wants for His creation? Be open to his reign. Want happiness and peace for yourself and others? Let God reign.

Talking, walking, and just *being* . . . Jesus embodied this Kingdom. If you want to know why Jesus healed, why Jesus forgave, why Jesus turned a laser eye to hypocrisy and opened his arms to the poor and to kids . . . that's why.

When God reigns . . .

The sick are healed, the blind see, and life breaks through.
Sins are forgiven, and you can start *all over again. Fresh. Clean. New.*

There's no such thing as an outcast. The lowly are raised up.

No one is hungry, no one is using other people, no one is stupid enough to build their lives on anything but the solid rock of God's love.

And creation is back—back to what God originally intended it to be, in all of its glory and wholeness.

This should help you see and hear Jesus in a whole new light. Too often we look at miracles, for example, and come away with this idea that Jesus performed miracles in order to prove to folks that he was divine.

Sorry, no.

Jesus performed miracles for the same reason that he did everything else — to bring God's reign into people's lives. Not to "show" or "prove" anything — but to *do it*. To *make it happen*.

Of course, the only way he, this man from Nazareth, could do such a thing was if he were, indeed, more than a man from Nazareth. Which is exactly what people began to suspect, without Jesus saying a word directly about it at first:

> And when he [Jesus] saw their faith he said, "Man, your sins are forgiven you." And the scribes and the Pharisees began to question, saying, "Who is this that speaks blasphemies? Who can forgive sins but God only?"
>
> Lk 5:20-21

Exactly.

True love

Finally, we're getting to it — what you thought this Jesus was all about, anyway.

Love.

And sure, he is. But . . . is it really that easy?

After all, what is love?

> Consider all of the ways we define love today:
>
> — wanting someone, emotionally and physically
>
> — caring about someone
>
> — enjoying someone's presence
>
> — being friends
>
> — being turned on
>
> — feeling happy, peaceful emotions
>
> How do these fall short? Let me count the ways. . . .

You see the problem, I trust. Once again, we're left swimming without a definition, open to anything and everything in the name of that thing called "love."

Here's what Jesus said about love:

"Love God . . . love your neighbor."

"No greater love . . ."

"God is love."

Now . . . what do these words of Jesus have to do with any of the definitions of love that our culture throws around and that we, too often, live by?

A little, here and there, sure. The caring part, at least. But if we're into letting God — not the culture — define love, here's what we've got.

Love isn't an emotion. It's an attitude, a stance, a way of life.

It's an attitude of care, concern, and compassion that puts the beloved's well-being before your own. It's an attitude of valuing the beloved, not for what they can do for us, but for who they are . . . just because . . . they are.

When it comes to loving other human beings, I've found this to be a really handy way of capturing everything Jesus said and did about love:

Since God is love, love is about seeing other human beings through God's eyes, as much as is humanly possible. It means treating them as God wants them to be treated. *As His beloved children . . . beloved as much as I am.*

No using. No exploitation. No revenge.

Just a brother or sister whose happiness and peace God desires as deeply as He desires mine.

That's love according to Jesus.

So since we're *Christians* . . . that's love according to us, too.

Love hurts

Here's the one part of Jesus' message you really don't hear much about.

The pain.

No wonder we try to keep it quiet. No one likes to talk about pain.

But it's there — sacrifice, suffering, and pain. Just like the Kingdom, just like love, it's all over the Gospels, too.

In fact, someone once said that the *only* thing that Jesus absolutely promised his disciples was that they would suffer. Not because he wanted them to, but because that's how the world usually responds when confronted by real love:

Shut it down. Quick.

Suffering is not something that Christians should seek — that's what we call masochism, and that's definitely not a good thing. But, Jesus makes clear again and again, being a disciple of his involves suffering.

And if you don't get it — look at a crucifix.

What is that all about? It's about following love through, no matter what pain it brings you. It's about the suffering that sin causes and the suffering that healing requires.

This is absolutely one of the hardest points of discipleship. Naturally enough, we try to avoid suffering, and our culture encourages that.

"Happiness" is usually defined, in some way, as the absence of suffering and pain, isn't it? Isn't that the goal of life the world lays before you right here, right now? Make enough money so you won't have to "suffer" mentally as you worry about where your second car is going to come from. Separate sex from love so you won't have to "suffer" as you pursue real, authentic intimacy with another person, and can just move on. Dull your senses with chemicals so you won't "suffer" from an inconvenient confrontation with your limitations, failures and mortality.

So sorry. It's not right, and ironically, it doesn't even work.

Look at it from a purely human standpoint. You should know by now that anything really good or important, any achievement or accomplishment, involves some level of suffering. No pain, no gain, etc. We seem to have little problem incorporating that truth into so many parts of our lives:

If we want to be in shape, we have to deny ourselves certain foods and go through the struggle of working out, which is not always fun, and which hurts.

If we want to achieve success in school or in our careers, most of us have to work hard, and we have to sacrifice something along the way—time, certain pleasures, immediate satisfaction—in favor of a long-term goal.

If we want to have firm, lasting friendships, we'll have to suffer. We'll have to grow through changes, work through disagreements, and sometimes even go our separate ways for a time.

If you're a creative person, you know about suffering, too. Sometimes ideas flow really easily, and your art or composition or writing is effortless, but sometimes—it's not. Sometimes, it's torture.

So yeah, we know about suffering, and its place in life.

But do we really?

Do we take it to the level Jesus calls us to?

Jesus is talking about and living on a different level than getting a better paycheck or a graduate degree or getting in shape. He's talking about *how to live* and where the deepest peace that you yearn for—and you know you do—is found.

And what he says is that suffering is a part of the package. It's different for every person. Your specific crosses are not mine. But we do all share a couple of common crosses:

*The challenge to really love, to see others and all of creation through God's eyes and act on it

*The truth and cold fact of the end of life on earth, and how we live in the face of it.

And here's the climax. Here's the end of the story—I'm not ruining it for you because you already know how it ends. But maybe you've never thought about it this way.

Putting God first, opening your life to his reign and throwing yourself into life with love, is going to involve suffering and sacrifice. It's going to bear down on you like a cross.

But you're not alone. You're not alone in your suffering, you're not alone in the journey, and most amazing of all, you're not alone in what you'll find on the other side.

Blessed are you.
Happy are you.
The tomb was empty.
Jesus stood before them and said:
Peace be with you.
And they were amazed.

CHAPTER 5

Always

So you, Jesus and a Bible.

Is that it? Is that all you need?

Some would say so.

But oddly enough, Jesus himself doesn't seem to be one of them.

Left behind

Perhaps by now, you've had a chance to read through a Gospel or two, or at least run your mind back through what you've heard before.

In the process, you might have noticed that one of the things Jesus constantly seems to be doing is *preparing* his disciples — preparing them for persecution, preparing them for suffering and rejection, and preparing them for his own death, his own physical departure from them.

The preparation for this final reality — his looming physical absence — usually takes the form of reassurance. John tells us, for example, that at the Last Supper, Jesus spent a lot of time trying to explain to his friends that they were intimately connected to him, and would stay that way, not to worry. Like branches connected to a vine, they were linked to him and therefore, to God. He tells them about the "Advocate" — the Holy Spirit, or the "Comforter" — who would be sent to dwell with them.

Matthew points to Jesus' continued presence with his apostles very directly, in a way that's hard to forget, especially since it's the last thing he quotes Jesus as saying:

"And behold, I am with you always, until the end of the age." (Mt 28:20)

So there you go. Jesus makes it clear that as his friends and disciples continued his ministry, they wouldn't be alone, either individually or — and this is important — as a community, as a group.

The most vivid, concrete expression of this, of course, broke into the disciples' lives the night before Jesus died, when they were gathered with him in a room in Jerusalem, threats swirling around them, mystery ahead of them.

That night they celebrated the ancient Passover meal, the meal in which Jews not only commemorate God's covenant and saving power, but, they believe, are brought in *touch* with it as well, in the here and now.

> And when the hour came, he sat at table, and the apostles with him. And he said to them, "I have earnestly desired to eat this passover with you before I suffer; for I tell you I shall not eat it until it is fulfilled in the kingdom of God." And he took a cup, and when he had given thanks he said, "Take this, and divide it among yourselves; for I tell you that from now on I shall not drink of the fruit of the vine until the kingdom of God comes." And he took bread, and when he had given thanks he broke it and gave it to them, saying, "This is my body which is given for you. Do this in remembrance of me." And likewise the cup after supper, saying, "This cup which is poured out for you is the new covenant in my blood."
>
> Lk 22:14-20

Jesus built on the meaning of this Passover meal, using his own life and coming death and resurrection as the core reality for them to touch and taste. He told his friends that the bread and wine were now more than they appeared — that they were his body and blood, his presence, a new covenant. And he told them to do what he was doing again, in memory of him. He wanted them to repeat the meal; whenever they did, they'd be in touch with his presence, wholly and entirely. He'd be with them in just the same way he was with them that night, amazingly enough. That's what we call Real Presence.

So, when you look at all of this together, and absorb everything Jesus was saying and doing, it's really clear that he was letting his disciples know that their identity was going to be a lot more than "followers of a dead guy's teaching," which is, unfortunately, all many of us think Church is.

No — it was more, something else, something deeper. It was "the community in which that guy still lives" and "the community where that guy can still be met, known and touched here and now."

That community. It's called the Church.

What "church" is and what it's not

A lot of us are turned off, or at the very least, bored by the whole idea — not to mention the experience — of church. We don't see the point: we go to church and we're struck by how out of touch the whole things seems with our lives, or we're actively turned off by things we see and words we hear . . . and we wonder why we "need" an institution when God is in our hearts all the time. So we separate ourselves, body and soul, from this institution that seems made by and for old people who, for some reason, actually *like* rules.

A valid reaction, maybe. I can't really argue with your feelings.

But I *can* tell you that your feelings are coming out of a totally inadequate understanding of the definition of "church."

So I guess that means I can argue with your feelings, after all.

When you read the New Testament (you are reading, aren't you?) with a totally open mind, you might be startled to find those

folks—Paul, Peter—the entire crop of Jesus' apostles, in fact—
don't seem to define "church" the same way we do. They don't
judge it by the same standards.

And incidentally, they cannot and do not try to conceive even
the possibility that one could be a "Christian" outside the context
of a Church. No *I'll go out in the woods and talk to Jesus on my own
on Sunday morning* for these guys.

A lot of us have somehow decided that "church" is like a club.
It's a gathering of like-minded folks, come together because they've
picked the same set of beliefs out of Aisle 6 at the Religion Super-
market.

Not only is it a club . . . it's also a *club.* In that we go expecting
to be entertained, stimulated, have our desires validated and our
needs met, and maybe even hook up.

No wonder we "can't get anything" out of 8:00 Mass at St.
Simeon Stylite Parish.

We're speaking a different language than—well, than the
Church is. We're thinking about church in a completely different
way than Christians have since New Testament times. Our expectations are totally out of whack with what Jesus formed his apostles to be and what they understood—*directly from him*—and
then recorded in the New Testament.

So let's decide. We'll root our judgment of what church is and
what role it should play in our lives in a definition of church.
Whose definition shall it be?

Ours?

Or Jesus'?

Body of Christ. Get it?

We've already laid out two basic definitions, you may have noticed.
The very, very common way of thinking about church today is as
a group of like-minded believers.

But Jesus indicates that the community of his disciples—the
Church—is defined not by *us* but by *him*. It's where *he is.*

Paul, the man who started out his adult life persecuting Christians and ended up martyred as one of them, did much to flesh out Jesus' meaning. Paul wasn't one of the original twelve apostles, but he argued strenuously for his right to be called an apostle because like The Twelve, he had been personally called by Jesus to follow him (1 Cor. 9:1-2).

He was called by Jesus on the road to Damascus where, as you remember, he was knocked off his horse and blinded for three days until he could see—and I mean *really see*—again. Then, his faith was formed by folks whose own faith was personally formed by Jesus himself. What he wrote in his letters, collected in the New Testament, reflects the very earliest Christian sense of what it means to be Church; a sense you can also see in the Acts of the Apostles, the record of early Christian life in Jerusalem, as well as the missionary travels of Paul.

So what, to these folks who were in touch with the source, is Church?

> * It's the Body of Christ. (Col 1:24, 1 Cor 12:27)
>
> * It's the Bride of Christ. (2 Cor 11:2, Eph 5:32)
>
> * It's the "household of God," the "dwelling place of God." (Eph 2:20-22)
>
> * It's established by Christ, and we're called to be a part of it—to be a part of *him*. (1 Pet 2:9)

Notice something, please. None of this seems to be primarily about us, does it? It's not about our journey, our story, or even (gasp!) our needs.

It's about *Jesus.*

Pull it all together, now:

Jesus came to reconcile, forgive and heal. He came to preach the Kingdom of God, and, even more than preach it—open it up to us, here and now.

Jesus—God made flesh, walking and talking just like us, born of the most amazing, sacrificial love—came to dwell among us to bring us into the amazing wholeness of God, and all He is: peace, truth, happiness, and blessing. Just the way God intended His creation to be all along.

Jesus didn't stop doing this after his death, resurrection and ascension into heaven.

He stayed—mysteriously, yet truly, as he *promised*—in the community of his apostles.

They—as a *community*, not as isolated individuals—were going to be the way that Jesus continued to be present on earth.

Through them—as they stayed tied to him like branches to a vine and were nourished by his presence—he'd keep preaching, healing, forgiving and loving, not just in a backwater of the Roman Empire now, but throughout the whole world.

The Body of Christ: his mouth, his hands, his feet, his loving heart.

Here. Now.

Losing my religion

Now let that sit and stew for a little bit. Ponder it.

This isn't just a different opinion, mind you. *This is what Church* is. *This is what Jesus and his apostles said it was—and is.*

So that definition is the *only* one we can legitimately go by as we make our decisions about our connection with Church.

Deal with it.

It's not "Am I sufficiently entertained?" or "Do I feel accepted by the congregation?" or "Do I feel like it?"

It's *"Do I want to be where Jesus is?"*

Because you know, you can do all kinds of singing and dancing about finding God on your own and needing no one and nothing else, but if you claim that Jesus is your Lord and you want to follow him . . . that road doesn't lead out into the woods alone. It just doesn't. That's totally alien to anything Jesus taught and the early Christians believed. For a Christian, there's no such thing as an individualistic faith.

It's all about belonging to Jesus and being nourished by him.

And as he himself makes it really, really clear — the place where that happens most concretely and most truly is within His Body, the Church.

It's a gift, really. Isn't it?

Yes, I know you might be used to thinking of church as a burden, an obligation, and a generally annoying place. But when you get into the Gospels, and then actually sit yourself down at Mass on Sunday, open to connecting the two at last — you just might get it.

Jesus lives. Jesus loves. He said he'd be with us, living and loving until the end of time. There are still tombs; there are still lonely, lost people wandering in them, left for dead by a fearful world. Still.

And guess where Jesus is?

Here. Now.

In and through His Body. Still.

CHAPTER 6

If You Must...

"I have to go to Mass in the morning."

"Do I have to go to Confession for this, or not?"

You might detect a theme.

A lot of us define our relationship to religious practice according to what we "have to" do. It's a matter of obligation, a matter of living by rules. It's about an institution that wants to keep us in the fold, bind us, and restrict our freedom.

This may be a common way of thinking, but does it have anything to do with the way things actually are?

And by clinging to it . . . could we be missing something?

Jesus, again

Yes, here we are, back again, listening to Jesus.

This book is about the good life—the life that each of us was created by God to lead. We've worked through a lot:

❋ If you buy the fact that you exist because God went to the trouble of creating you out of love, then it makes sense that when we're looking for fulfillment in this life He gave—we turn to Him. God knows.

❋ God, being that loving God, didn't leave us orphaned. He gave us the capacity to know and listen to Him. It's in the gift of Jesus that we find that gift the most concretely expressed, the most accessible. Which makes sense, because that's probably the reason God came to us as one of us: to be accessible.

❋ Jesus, God made flesh, walked on the same earth we do and spoke our language (the language of human beings, that is). We have lots of questions about how to live life — Jesus really is the answer.

❋ If we're serious about figuring this out and grabbing that good life, we'll get to know Jesus — *really* know him, now, as adults. We're not going to rely on hazy memories of what someone tried to teach us in eighth grade. We're going to read Scripture and pray, because a stranger can't become a friend unless you take the trouble to talk to him.

❋ Jesus, God's gift of himself, leaves yet another gift: his continuing presence, here and now, in the Church. We don't have to wander and wonder — he *said* he would be present here, and *he is.*

❋ If you want to stay connected and be nourished by Jesus' sure presence, and if you want your life to be *good* — separating yourself from the presence of Jesus in his Church is *not* something you're going to consider.

The next question is . . . how?

When I'm looking at my Church today, when I'm trying to find the place where I can know Jesus and be touched by him . . . what should I be looking for?

Branches, meet Vine

What began with Jesus and his apostles in Jerusalem has grown, over two thousand years, into something that's almost unbelievably rich. If your experience of Catholic life has ranged all the way from the St. Aloysius Parish School to the college student center, and you think that there's nothing more to being Catholic than that — think again.

It's through this Body of Christ that the Good News we talked about earlier has spread to every corner of the earth. Nourished by the presence of the living Jesus, his disciples have healed bodies and souls, dwelt with the poor, embraced the outcast, stood up to oppression, educated young and old, sat quietly with the dying, and listened to the weeping repentant sinner.

Not to mention composed breathtaking music, created astonishing works of art, built cathedrals, expanded scientific knowledge, and brought peace into warring lands.

Even today, no single institution educates more children or tends to more sick and dying people than the Catholic Church. Monks and nuns still live among us, welcoming strangers, praying for us all. Every day, broken lives begin the long journey to wholeness, a journey that begins because someone is letting Jesus' love work through them.

What binds all of this together? What makes it one? What unifies all of this good work, this care, this healing, this creativity?

Jesus, of course. Because it's all flowing from his Body, the Church, continuing his ministry.

And no matter what era or what part of the globe you look at, even though you might find differences in worldview or particular traditions, the one point that binds us all to one another and to Jesus is this:

The sacramental life of the Church.

Yup. All those things you think you "have to" do.

Turns out their purpose and power runs a little deeper than some of us thought.

Lifelines

Sacraments are nothing new to you. You can probably define and list them easily. You probably even know that they are central to a Catholic's religious practice.

But do you know why?

It's not because they're badges of membership or stepping-stones to maturity.

It's because through sacraments, *Jesus acts.*

Think about it. During his earthly ministry, Jesus called people to follow him and join themselves to him in the deepest kind of life with God.

(Baptism, anyone?)

Jesus, much to the shock and scandal of others, actually forgave sins.

(It's called Reconciliation.)

Jesus shared his very self — God's self — with his disciples, nourishing them, strengthening them, and pulling them into the heavenly banquet.

(Bread of Life. Eucharist. Communion. Every day, if you choose.)

Jesus acts through the other sacraments as well . . . gives us the Holy Spirit (Confirmation), calls us to ministry (Holy Orders), joins us in marriage (Matrimony), and pours out God's healing, according to his will (Anointing of the Sick).

It makes a lot of sense, when you think about it. The Church is the Body of Christ, and in these sacraments, Christ's Body — Jesus — acts, and continues his earthly ministry, which is exactly what he intended it to do:

> For just as the body is one and has many members, and all the members of the body, though many, are one body, so it is with Christ. For by one Spirit we were all baptized into one body — Jews or Greeks, slaves or free — and all were made to drink of one Spirit.
>
> If one member suffers, all suffer together; if one member is honored, all rejoice together. Now you are the body of Christ and individually members of it. And God has appointed in the church first apostles, second prophets, third teachers, then workers of miracles, then healers, helpers, administrators, speakers in various kinds of tongues. Are all apostles? Are all prophets? Are all teachers? Do all

work miracles? Do all possess gifts of healing? Do all speak with tongues? Do all interpret? But earnestly desire the higher gifts. And I will show you a still more excellent way.

1 Cor 12:12-13, 26-31

We're going to look at three of these sacraments more closely, but before we do, let's bring it all together:

Jesus is the answer to your questions and the end of your quest. He's not absent. He's present. Yes, he's present in your heart and life all the time, and we deepen our knowledge of him through reading the Gospels and praying, but . . .

He leaves us something just a little more certain, solid and sure, as well. He knew that our understanding of Scripture can be limited, and all kinds of distractions and temptations can muffle his voice when we are just praying on our own. He knows that we can wonder, "Is it God I'm really hearing, or just my imagination or my needs?" He knows that we're human, in other words.

That just as in our human relationships, we need the concrete; we need the moments in which we are really present to one another, in which we can look into another person's eyes and hear a voice. We know and trust that our relationship is real and good — but we still need those moments of *presence* in which it's embodied, confirmed, and expressed.

There's something else about being human: as human beings, in fact, is how Jesus meets us. He doesn't meet us as ghosts or as pure spirits because, well, that's not what we are. He takes on flesh and meets us as creatures with bodies and souls. During his earthly ministry, people were changed by Jesus through his presence, through his touch, his words, over meals, surrounded by the good, basic stuff of this earth: bread, wine, oil, water and even mud — dirt mixed with Jesus' own saliva (Jn 9:6-7).

Nothing's changed.

(Except maybe the saliva part — but you never know.)

CHAPTER 7

Hooking Up

In the most ancient Christian traditions, seven specific sacraments — concrete moments of Jesus' actions among us, moments in which his grace is poured out just as it was on those he touched in Galilee — have been recognized.

We're going to look at three of them in some detail, because they're the three that touch your life the most profoundly and frequently:

Baptism, Eucharist, and Reconciliation.

Identity, nourishment, and renewal.

The basics of life we come to, again and again.

Born — again

You might have been asked, once or twice in your life, if you were saved, if you've given your life to Christ.

Hope you said yes — because, you know, you were.

It happened when you were baptized. Okay, you may not remember it, and you may want to object because it wasn't your decision . . .

But was it your decision to be born in the first place? Do you have serious objections to that reality that wasn't in your control? Hope not.

It's all a mystery — an organic, deep, rich mystery. But if you're glad that God, working through the needs and desires and odd timing of your parents, brought you into being, perhaps you can work up a bit of gratitude that in the same way, He called you into a deeper relationship with Him when people who loved you were moved to get you baptized.

Baptism is, of course, the rite through which we are joined to the Church. But perhaps by now, several chapters into this book, you have a sense that this means something more than the crossing-over ceremony my sons went through from Tiger to Cub Scouts.

If the Church is, above all else, the community which Jesus called together and in which he dwells — if it is, as we say, His Body — then baptism really is the moment in which we're . . . saved. It's the moment in which our lives are transformed because they're absorbed into his.

> Jesus answered, "Truly, truly, I say to you, unless one is born of water and the Spirit, he cannot enter the kingdom of God. That which is born of the flesh is flesh, and that which is born of the Spirit is spirit."
>
> Jn 3:5-6

Not that the good life is, from that point on, guaranteed. It's not magic we're talking about here. Lots of things can go wrong, even complete and total wrong turns. Plenty of people who've been baptized have ended up, tragically, far from God.

Why? Because, as we have to keep reminding ourselves, we're human beings. If someone stands in front of you holding a gift, you have a choice. You can accept or reject it. If you reject it, of course that gift won't have any impact on your life except as a memory of what could have been.

The power and effect of that gift on your life depends on your receptivity, your openness . . . what you do with it.

So it is with the grace of baptism. Grace — that's a word that essentially means God's life within you — is poured out on you, bringing you into God's embrace at your baptism. Literally — into the arms of the Body of Christ, dying, rising, and alive forever.

BAPTISM: WHAT IT IS

Christians baptize because Jesus told us to (Mt 28:19). It's the fundamental way we're joined to him, and has been understood that way from earliest Christianity. To get even more specific, through baptism:

* Sins are forgiven (Acts 2:38)

* We're reborn in Christ (2 Cor 5:17, Jn 3:5)

* We're incorporated into the Body of Christ (Eph 4:25)

Hungry?

Mass is a big deal and a constant topic of conversation for Catholics. We wonder why we should go and how often. Once we're in the seat, we look around, listen, and find plenty to complain about. We leave and we wonder what we got out of it and (again) when we have to go back.

Do you think we've missed the point?

Look. Catholic worship is rich and complex. Our experience of it is definitely affected by a lot of purely human factors — how we feel that day, the quality of the music and the preaching, whether we feel connected to the community or not, and more.

That's okay, too, up to a point. After all, as I kept saying to you a few paragraphs ago, we're human beings with bodies and senses. God wants to reach us through those bodies any way He can — and He does. The experience of beauty, for example, can bring us closer to God because God is the perfection of beauty and truth. That's why, over the centuries, Catholics have put such an emphasis on art and music. The environment in which we worship can, and probably even should, draw us closer to the presence of God, who is beauty and truth.

But there is another side to this, a side that has the power to really damage our relationship with God and our experience of worship. It's what happens when we let the externals of liturgy, and secondary definitions of what Catholic worship is all about, completely take over our expectations and experience . . . getting in the way instead of opening the gate.

To get this, think about the reasons you've offered, over the years, to skip Mass or at least diminish its role in your life. It's boring. Same thing over and over. Awful, lame, wretched music. Homilies that have nothing to do with your life. Cold, lifeless congregations.

Now — think again.

Think about what the Mass *is,* at its root, at its foundation.

> Whoever, therefore, eats the bread or drinks the cup of the Lord in an unworthy manner will be guilty of profaning the body and blood of the Lord. Let a man examine himself, and so eat of the bread and drink of the cup. For any one who eats and drinks without discerning the body eats and drinks judgment upon himself.
>
> 1 Cor 11:27-29

Connecting with the presence of Jesus — *that's* the essence of what happens at Mass. Everything else exists to focus on that and build on it.

In other words, short and sweet — *Mass isn't about your emotions.*

It's about connecting with Jesus. It's about doing this as individuals and as a community. It's about expressing our identity as the Body of Jesus and thanking God for this gift. It's about the heavenly banquet of intimacy with God, offered right here, right now.

Is that why you go to Mass?

Even close?

So let's try something. Let's forget about the "have tos" and the rules, and let's think, instead, in terms of gift. Let's imagine that God actually knows what your needs are, knows your yearnings, and has answered every one. Here. Now.

You sit in your room and try to pray. You wonder . . . is it God I'm talking to, or just myself?

You ache for some sure sign of God's presence in your life and in your world.

You read the Gospels, and you want to be in touch with the Jesus you read about there, the Jesus who loves, heals, comforts, and can make you whole.

Wonder no more.

"Have to" go to Mass?

How in the world can you stay away?

So sorry

One of the weirdest things about Catholics, according to those who aren't, is this sacrament we call Reconciliation, and which our parents called Confession.

Why confess to a priest? Why do we . . . (here we go again) . . . have to do that?

Why not just keep it between you and God? What's wrong with that?

Well, the bottom line is that all of your sins and failures *are* between you and God. Even the most scrupulous, neurotic person in the world isn't going to be able to confess every nook and cranny of her life in this sacrament, nor does the Church even suggest that. Every day should have at least one moment in which we stop, look honestly at what we've done, said and thought about, present the failures to God, ask for forgiveness and be renewed. We have prayers just for that purpose:

ACT OF CONTRITION

O my God, I am heartily sorry for having offended you, and I detest all my sins because of your just punishments; but most of all, because they offend you, my God, who are all good and deserving of all my love. I firmly resolve with the help of your grace to sin no more, and to avoid the near occasion of sin.

But there are some cold, hard facts about human beings, these creatures that God made and knows so well:

It's really hard for us sometimes to let go of our sins.

It's hard to believe that we're really and truly forgiven.

It's hard to believe that we can really start over again.

It's hard for us not to define ourselves by our past sins and mistakes.

Sometimes we can reach that level of assurance just in the privacy of our own heads and hearts — but not always.

It's the way it is with human relationships, and it's the way it is with us and God. We need the voice, we need to hear assurance that all is well — we need the direct, personal contact that brings us back from the little graves we've dug for ourselves.

And just like that — the gift is given.

On the evening of that day, the first day of the week, the doors being shut where the disciples were, for fear of the Jews, Jesus came and stood among them and said to them, "Peace be with you." When he had said this, he showed them his hands and his side. Then the disciples were glad when they saw the Lord. Jesus said to them again, "Peace be with you. As the Father has sent me, even so I send you." And when he had said this, he breathed on them, and said to them, "Receive the Holy Spirit. If you forgive the sins of any, they are forgiven; if you retain the sins of any, they are retained."

Jn 20:19-23

So . . . do we "have to?"

Wrong question. Again.

Sure, there are some sins so deep that they really do wound our relationship to God, the Body of Christ, and creation pretty profoundly, sins that bring our souls closer to death. Mortal (deadly) sins, we call them. Just as some personal crises require more outside help and intervention than others, so it is with those sins. If you've broken the bonds of love in a serious way, it calls for serious repair. With those kinds of sins, you really do "have to" reconcile yourself to the community you've damaged.

But on a broader level, this question of "have to" just really misses the point, doesn't it?

It's just like every other contact point with Jesus we've talked about in this chapter. During his earthly ministry, people ran to Jesus, looking for forgiveness and healing. They defied family, friends, the disapproval of religious authorities, and social conventions just to touch and be touched by Jesus and hear the fantastic, amazing news that they were forgiven, and they didn't have to live with their sin for one more second.

> One of the Pharisees asked him to eat with him, and he went into the Pharisee's house, and took his place at table. And behold, a woman of the city, who was a sinner, when she learned that he was at table in the Pharisee's house, brought an alabaster flask of ointment, and standing behind him at his feet, weeping, she began to wet his feet with her tears, and wiped them with the hair of her head, and kissed his feet, and anointed them with the ointment. Now when the Pharisee who had invited him saw it, he said to himself, "If this man were a prophet, he would have known who and what sort of woman this is who is touching him, for she is a sinner." And Jesus answering said to him, "Simon, I have something to say to you." And he answered, "What is it, Teacher?" "A certain creditor had two debtors; one owed five hundred denarii, and the other fifty. When they could not pay, he forgave them both. Now which of them

will love him more?" Simon answered, "The one, I suppose, to whom he forgave more." And he said to him, "You have judged rightly." Then turning toward the woman he said to Simon, "Do you see this woman? I entered your house, you gave me no water for my feet, but she has wet my feet with her tears and wiped them with her hair. You gave me no kiss, but from the time I came in she has not ceased to kiss my feet. You did not anoint my head with oil, but she has anointed my feet with ointment. Therefore I tell you, her sins, which are many, are forgiven, for she loved much; but he who is forgiven little, loves little." And he said to her, "Your sins are forgiven." Then those who were at table with him began to say among themselves, "Who is this, who even forgives sins?" And he said to the woman, "Your faith has saved you; go in peace."

Lk 7:36-50

They didn't meet Jesus, listen to him, and mutter, "Hey, do I *have* to go to this guy to be forgiven?"

They couldn't stay away.

Jump up to here and now.

What's on your mind? Your soul? What horrible habits (aka demons) do you know you should want — and really *do* want — to be freed from? What destructive roads seem inevitable for you? What's hanging over your head? What are you feeling guilty about? What are you guilty of?

It doesn't have to be that way, you know. The slate can be cleaned, the road can be straightened, the darkness can be driven away.

It's what Jesus did then.

It's what Jesus is doing now — through His Body, the Church. In that gift he's given, a gift that may seem strange to the outsider, but makes perfect sense once you've actually listened to Jesus and get what it's all about.

And like I said before . . . once you get that . . . how can you stay away?

CHAPTER 8

Say Your Prayers

Life changes.

Good thing, too.

It would be frightening and a little sad if you saw life exactly the same way now as you did when you were thirteen. If you related to your parents now just as you related to them when you were ten. Or if you thought through problems in the same framework as you did when you were sixteen.

Or prayed the same way . . .

Oh.

The more things change . . .

. . . the more they stay the same.

And there are actually a few qualities of our childhood prayer life that are worth retaining into adulthood.

As a child, you probably brought an attitude of trust and hope to your prayer. You couldn't articulate why or how it worked, but just as you trusted your parents to know you, love you, and take care of your needs, you trusted God in the same way.

Your prayer was probably amazingly honest, even to the point of being a little strange sometimes. Kids, as a rule, don't hold back when they pray, because kids don't hold back when they talk, period. Whatever pops into their head — they lay it out before God. For years, when I was small, I kept praying for this kitten that had gotten stuck in a tree in my grandmother's neighborhood. My son David once prayed for Beethoven to get his hearing back.

What's implicit in those prayers is faith that God is God — that He loves you so much, no prayer is too strange to be spoken and that He can, indeed do anything.

Is all of that still in your heart when you pray? Or has some of it been lost along the way, smothered by over-thinking, cynicism and doubt of God's power and love?

Well, you might want to work on that.

But not everything should be the same as it was.

So what should be different? Pretty much the qualities that are different in your normal everyday communication with those closest to you:

QUALITIES OF AN ADULT'S PRAYER:

* You don't just talk . You listen.

* You understand that you're not the center of the universe, and that others have needs as well.

* You get that the point of all of this is a deeper relationship, and you're willing to do whatever it takes to reach that point.

* You're willing to grow, admit mistakes and try new ways of communicating even more honestly .

* You understand that the point, ultimately, isn't getting what you want, but being the person you were created to be . . . and you're willing to just be in the presence of the One who made you, so you can be that very person.

That's it: You want to relate to God as an adult? Keep the trust, the faith, the awe, and the love. Bring in the quiet, the listening, the openness, the humility, and the Big Picture.

Now. Say your prayers. Okay?

What is it?

What is prayer, anyway? Time for a refresher course, perhaps?

The most important thing to remember about prayer is that it's all actually shockingly simple: Prayer is simply being consciously in the presence of God.

That's really it.

If you read the great Christian spiritual teachers, they'll tell you the same thing. The "height" of Christian prayer is contemplation — the wordless, awe-filled stillness in God's presence, in which it is just you and the Creator of the Universe, being present. Which means, of course, being in the Presence of Love, Truth, Beauty, and Eternity, because that's Who God is.

But, like anything simple, it's a lot harder than it looks.

If you can, observe a couple who've been married, say, sixty years or so and are still devoted to each other. Their relationship looks lovely in its simplicity. As you watch them relate, wordlessly sometimes, you might even be tempted to call it all very "contemplative." But then just ask them about it. Ask them — "Was the road to this point simple, uncomplicated and easy?"

Get ready to be laughed off your park bench with that one.

It's the same with God. God is God, and we are incredibly limited human beings. The deepest yearnings of your heart are drawing you to unending and unchanging joy, peace and life. Every time you pray you bring that yearning to the surface. But that same heart is limited, wears blinders, is selfish and shortsighted.

So instant, deep contemplation and ecstatic union with God probably won't happen for you immediately. Just as it didn't for that old couple. It took years of talking, listening, yelling, laughing, changing and even (we don't like to admit it) suffering.

But if you don't start . . . when are you ever going to get there?

St. Teresa of Ávila, a great, earthy and funny 17th-century mystic and spiritual teacher, said that prayer "means taking time frequently conversing in secret with Him Who, we know, loves us," and she's absolutely right. But just try to be that and do that completely on your own, right now.

Well?

What you might have found are all sorts of roadblocks. You want to think about God, but you're distracted by the low numbers that are called your bank account, or the puzzling comment your boss dropped at work. You want to talk to God, but you don't know what to say. You want to listen to God, but you don't know how to shut off your own brain, and when you do manage to actually listen . . . you're not sure if it's God you're hearing, your own imagination, your needs, or even echoes of your dad's voice, still ringing in your conscience from way back when.

And then there's time. That little thing. Who has it?

Prayer: simple, but not. Because we're not.

Help!

But here's the thing.

You want that good life? Here and now? You want that connection with the Lord that you know and believe will fill you with peace?

It's not going to happen if you don't pray. Early and often. It really is exactly like a friendship or love relationship — something deep and important doesn't happen without time and energy. Not with friends, girlfriends, boyfriends, parents, children, spouses, or God.

We know it.

Now — can we *live it?*

CHAPTER 9

Where? What? How?

Yes we can —live it, that is. We want to, as well.

But where do we start?

What do we say when we pray as adults?

And how can we listen to God—not as little kids, but as adults really interested in intimacy with the One who shaped us, knows us, and loves us?

Don't worry. It's been done. It's happened. Dig deep into the experiences of Christians who've prayed before you were even born, and you'll find something. You'll find a lot of joy—maybe exactly what you're looking for.

Where to start

Everyone is different, it's true. One person's way of communicating with God isn't going to be another person's. Reading the wisdom of great Catholic spiritual teachers, you see how true this is. St. Louis de Montfort was a huge rosary fan. St. Thérèse of Lisieux admitted she could barely get through the rosary. St. Ignatius, in his *Spiritual Exercises*, emphasized the use of the imagination in prayer. Others, like St. John of the Cross, were starker in their approach.

But what's also true is that for Catholics, there are actually a few starting points that have been proven trustworthy for just about everyone. You may end up going in different directions, preferring one type of meditation or devotion over another — heaven knows, the Catholic tradition is rich enough to have something for everyone — but right here, in the beginning, it's a really good idea to trust the experience of two thousand years.

Why?

From listening to some, you might think that starting with these tried-and-true basics of Catholic prayer is important because it's what gives you what they call a "Catholic identity." Or what ties you to the Church. Or what you (here we go again) *have to do* in order to be considered a Catholic. Because these are the things that Catholics do. So if you want to be in the club . . .

Nope. Stop it.

Think reasonably about it. There are certain ways of praying and moments of prayer that Catholics have relied on for two thousand years. Why do you think this is? Do you really think it's because of rules requiring the mindless millions throughout the centuries to conform or else?

Or could it be . . . because these not-so-mindless millions have found these words, ways, and moments . . . helpful?

Or to put it more bluntly: because they *work?*

I hate to use that word in this context, but I think you know what I mean: these traditions and practices are the root of Catholic prayer because through them . . . *people have found intimacy and friendship with God.*

So maybe — just maybe — you could trust their experience, and give it a shot yourself.

And start with the source so many of them found to be a rich well of joy: Mass.

Really. The next time you go to Mass, try this:

Pray.

Yup. Don't wonder who's there and who's not. Don't dumbly stare at people as they come back from Communion. Don't check out what everyone's wearing. Don't even indulge in a mental checklist of what's lame and what's not about this particular priest or this particular group of musicians.

Pray.

So ... when the priest asks us to call to mind our sins and ask God for forgiveness at the beginning ...

Pray. For forgiveness.

When you sing "Alleluia" before the Gospel, remember that it means "Praise God" and ... *pray.* In praise of God for your life, all of creation, and all of the weird, wonderful things that happened to you in the last few days.

When you listen to the readings, open your heart and mind, and *pray.*

When you're praying for the needs of the community, lift up your own needs — from that bank account to the fears that hit you like a brick in the middle of the night — and those of whom you love, and ... *pray.*

When you're led into the mystery of Jesus' sacrifice and Real Presence ... pray. You've been seeking and wondering and hoping to be closer to God. Well, here he is. Here. Now. *Pray.*

Will you?

I don't mean engage in an interior monologue, jabbering away. That's not prayer. It's what St. Therese says: turning your eyes and heart to God. Be. With. God.

So yes. Start there. And maybe, if you're really intent on this, find an additional Mass during the week to go to. You know, going to Mass more than once a week — it's been done. By many. Early in the morning, at lunch, in the evening. Odds are there's a parish somewhere near you that offers daily Mass at a time when you can hit it, at least once during the week.

Lots and lots of folks have found this an invaluable moment of real prayer in the busy-ness of their daily lives. To be honest, they sometimes find daily Mass a little bit more conducive to prayer than the possibly very crowded Sunday liturgy. Try it.

Using the Mass as the starting point to a deeper life of prayer makes sense because it's ancient, it's tested and true, and *it's there.* After all, you're going there anyway.

Right?

Say your prayers

So yes, start with really praying when you go to Mass.

But there's more...

Jewish and Christian spiritual practices differ, but they do share an awful lot, which makes sense, since one evolved from the other. One of the points of similarity is an understanding of the importance of praying regularly and habitually in the morning and in the evening.

So, if you're really interested in getting closer to God, there's your second step, right there. Start your day with prayer and end it the same way. Why? Because it's been done? Because it's "traditional?" No... turn that around. Maybe it's "traditional" because people find it helpful and nourishing and life giving—you know, to start your day remembering who you came from and end it remembering where you're going.

At the rising and the setting of the sun . . .

To get into the habit of morning and evening prayer, try one of these suggestions:

* Memorize a traditional morning or evening prayer from a Catholic prayer book.

* Pray a shortened version of the Church's Morning or Evening Prayer. The monthly publication *Magnificat* is a good source for this.

> * Pray the full Morning or Evening Prayer. You can find it online,
> or from volumes of the Liturgy of the Hours found at any
> Catholic bookstore.

Not to mention grace before meals, thanksgiving after meals, maybe a prayer at lunch . . .

The fact is, for centuries Catholics marked their days by set periods of prayer, no matter how brief. Not everyone followed the exact same pattern or prayed identical words, but when you look at the lives of ordinary folk in the cities and countryside of heavily Catholic countries, when you look at the lives of monks and nuns . . . you see it. Prayer in the morning, noon and night, and a few points in between.

A lot of us react against the suggestion of structuring and committing to prayer time. We want it to be all natural and spontaneous, and we think that it's somehow more "real" that way.

Once again, try out that relationship analogy. Even when someone is quite important to you, you have to structure time with them. If you're in a relationship for a while, you may find it necessary to remind yourself to say certain things or shut up at certain times, not to labor under the delusion that spontaneity is the key to helping that relationship grow.

Face it. We're all so busy we *have* to structure our time. You know, for example, how easy it is to fall out of the habit of working out. It's something that's important to you, something that you know is good for you, and once you get into the habit and rhythm, you actually sort of, kind of start to enjoy it.

But for most of us, getting to that point requires commitment to go to the gym . . . at this hour on this day, no matter what, no matter how we feel.

In relationships, we can get to the point where we assume that the other person will always be there, or that things between us are fine, and that we really don't have to work, plan, or make time, or be conscious of how we treat that person . . .

Until you wake up one morning and realize that . . . things just aren't like they were. And they sure aren't good.

So yeah, we get it with the rest of life. Structure is not evil. We need it. God's no different. At any given moment, we can think of a million different things we'd rather do than sit down and face God with our true selves in prayer. Structure, habit, and commitment bring us back — and make it harder for us to avoid that real self.

And admit it — your day is structured, anyway, isn't it? You have a work schedule. You structure your time around certain events, whether that be a game, a concert, or just your nightly dose of *South Park.*

Why not let time with God be a point of structure, too?

What would be wrong with that?

What could you possibly lose?

That's not worth losing anyway, that is.

Our Father

Let's step back and remember what all of this is for.

God is real and a part of your life. It's in Him — in love that never ends and truth that never fails — that you're going to find joy that lasts.

Prayer brings us into that space where we can really listen to God and be held by Him.

In some ways prayer is simple; it's just being present to God. In other ways, it's complicated, just as any relationship is complicated. There are tons of temptations to confront and weaknesses to deal with. Praying during Mass is a good place to start growing that prayer life. Structuring prayer moments during your day is another.

But what will you say during those moments?

Anything that's on your mind, first off. There's nothing you can't say to God — just be prepared for the answer. If you're saying, "Gee, I can't concentrate on prayer because I'm so worried about school," catch a clue. Maybe *you should be praying about school, then.* Most of the time, the stuff that's in our head "distracting us" from prayer isn't a distraction at all.

It's what we need to be bringing to God in the first place.

As I mentioned before, there is no shortage of prayer traditions and styles in Catholicism. If you want to meditate, for example, you don't have to turn to Eastern religions. Explore your own tradition first — not because we're scared of what you'll find over there, but because, frankly, Eastern, non-Christian meditation has a different purpose than Christian meditation. The former really is trying to get you to a place of forgetting your individual self; the latter is about bringing that individual self into deeper relationship with God. One is really anti-personal; the other is intensely personal.

But if you're new at this, it really might be a good idea for you to frame the very individual yearnings of your own heart within the strength and wisdom of traditional Catholic vocal prayer. You know — Our Fathers, Hail Marys, the Morning Offering, the Anima Christi, and the Psalms.

It's something we might resist, or might not even think of at all. Aren't those kinds of prayers for little kids or for people who don't have the guts to face God on their own?

No. Unless you'd like to suggest that every great spiritual teacher in the Catholic tradition was a gutless, childish wonder when it came to God.

The fact is, every one of those great spiritual teachers understood better than you or I that while the heart of prayer is you and God, gazing at each other in purity and love, all of those human weaknesses can wreck havoc on our plans for mystical union, and traditional vocal prayers are absolutely necessary to keep us on track.

Look at it this way:

Say you're angry at someone or at a situation. How do you bring that to prayer?

You might start out ranting and raving, and maybe by the end of your few minutes of prayer on the subject, you've reached a level of calmness, if only through sheer emotional exhaustion.

But . . . *have you grown? Have you been able to shut up your own emotions and listen to God?*

Or did you just descend into a puddle of self-pity?

Now contemplate an alternative scenario.

You bring your anger to God, but frame it with some traditional vocal prayers. Maybe you say the Our Father, slowly, before and after you talk and (try to) listen to God.

Forgive us our trespasses, as we forgive those . . .

Or you dig deeper and come up with a traditional prayer attributed to St. Patrick:

Christ with me, Christ before me . . . Christ in the mouth of everyone who speaks to me, Christ in the heart of everyone who thinks of me . . .

Or, you even let your anger drop away for a bit, as you look at a crucifix and repeat a basic prayer of Eastern Christians:

Jesus, Son of the Living God, have mercy on me a sinner.

Now. Do you see?

You want peace and joy in your life, but you just can't get there if you depend solely on your own words and thought processes. A huge part of prayer is letting yourself be shaped by God and His love. These prayers express the destination. They take our random, scattershot needs, wants, and hopes, and point them in the direction of hope and peace. Not just in eternity, but here and now.

It's not a matter of rattling off words. It's not a matter of having a rosary in your pocket because That's What Catholics Do. It's about trusting the experiences of millions of folks who have lived, loved, and suffered on the same earth you're walking right now. Trusting that if they found deeper intimacy with God through the use of these prayers . . . maybe you can too.

Try it.

Who's talking now

So far, we've focused on the concrete — when to pray, what words to say, what temptations you're going to face.

Let me finish up with a bit about attitude.

Communication can be tough, period. You can have someone you know very well stand in front you, have a conversation with you, and then walk away, leaving you wondering, "What was she saying? What did she mean?"

And communicating with God can be the same way. Actually, it's not our half of the conversation that puzzles us — it's God's. How do we know what God is saying to us? How can we recognize God's voice? How can we sift out God's will from all of the other voices in our heads?

There aren't any black and white rules to bring to this. But there are some guidelines that you might find helpful. Guidelines for attitudes to bring to your prayer life that will help you *discern* (that's the word we use) what God's saying and what He definitely isn't.

First, when you come to prayer, you have to be totally open to God's will. You can't be thinking that the purpose of this is to change God's mind about your life. You have to be ready to accept whatever God says.

Second, when you do sense that something or someone is calling you in a certain direction, you need to do some comparison shopping. Is what you're feeling consistent with what God says about life and truth in the Scriptures and in the teaching of the Church?

If it's not — if you're feeling a really deep pull to lash out in revenge, for example — you can be pretty certain that's not from God, because it contradicts Jesus' words in the Gospels. And just like that, you have another starting point for real, deeper prayer — not just your own emotions, but your own emotions and life bounced off what God's revealed about it all. You're not alone in your own head when it comes to figuring out God's will. He's given us directions, and we're allowed to use them.

Finally, it's about peace, and by that I mean real peace and real joy. When you live out what you sense God is telling you . . . what's the fruit? And not just for you, but for others, as well?

Do you feel really at peace? Have your actions brought real love into the hearts and lives of others? Is everything whole?

Because that's the point, you know, the point of all of this prayer: to find that wholeness and peace in the here and now. When you pray honestly and selflessly, you've opened yourself to that place in a way that's just not possible otherwise.

God's in that place.

And He's waiting.

SECTION II

The Good Life

CHAPTER 10

Life Before Death

We'll begin this chapter and section on an especially cheery note: *Memento Mori.*

Or: Remember. You're going to die.

So. How's your day going?

Am I lying?

Well, am I? No. It's the unavoidable truth — you are going to die someday. Your physical life on earth is going to end with either a bang or a whimper, the people who love you will gather, weep, and remember, and your body will be lowered into the ground.

It's not the end, of course, so don't get too depressed. It's all an entrance to something better — the fulfillment of all that's gone before, the gift of eternal life, in the eternal here and now with the God who created you just for this:

> "O death, where is thy victory? O death, where is thy sting?"
>
> 1 Cor 15:55

But the mysterious and puzzling thing is that our lives don't just begin there, in heaven. God puts us on this planet first, in the midst of all of the complexities, challenges, and oddness that define life on earth.

I don't presume to understand the depths of God's reasoning on this matter (or any matter), but it does seem to lead to an important point:

The years you spend on earth mean something.

After all, God could have just made us all angels, spiritual beings who never had to grow, change, get a job, lose a friend, get sick, and age.

But He didn't. And the fact that He didn't — that our life in eternity is preceded by life on earth — says something about this time we've been given.

What?

I, Not Robot

When you listen to what pop culture says about life beyond death, you notice something, pretty consistently:

Pop culture would have you believe that it's all just automatic — that one thing leads to another, and everyone who lives on earth just naturally steps into the next stage of paradise without skipping a beat or paying a price.

Comforting on one level, perhaps, but really based on nothing except wishful thinking and *not at all what God himself has revealed about life after death.*

Look. You can read all of the modern speculations about life after death that you like, but the fact remains — it's all speculation. As a Christian, your trust is in Jesus. Think back to the first section of this book, in which we laid out the basis of our faith — it's in the fact of *Jesus risen and alive.*

That's the center of our thinking about eternal life — not some vague notion of "whatever your deepest desires are" or something like that. It's about our real flesh and blood, transformed by God into lives and bodies that will live in perfect joy forever. Jesus showed us. The apostles saw it and gave their lives to that truth.

And it's about this:

Life before death has consequences for life after death.

Now, you might be used to thinking about all of this in terms of rewards and punishments, and once again, I must ask you to stop it. This isn't about breaking rules. It's about how you live your life. In short:

What you say "yes" to on earth . . . is what you're saying "yes" to for eternity.

In other words, since life after death is all about life with God, the journey there is obviously about saying yes to . . . God.

After all . . . why would you want to spend eternity with someone you've spent your life rejecting?

This isn't about God sending you anywhere just because He feels like it that day. It's about your decisions, your choices, and your response to God's call to you in your heart.

You're not a robot. You're a person with an absolute free will. God made you that way so your life and choices would mean something, would resonate, would make you, quite frankly, more like Him, if you want them to.

There's a purpose to this life you have. It's about finding joy now and, as a consequence, finding joy forever.

If you choose.

Not alone . . .

Don't get the idea that you're alone on this journey or even that you have the power to save yourself. Sure, you can do a lot of things — like make a fundamental choice about the direction of your life, but there are a lot of things you need God — God's grace for — as you go.

* You can't forgive yourself.

* You don't have the strength, completely on your own, to follow Jesus. That's a hard road. You need grace.

> * The strength to live any of the virtues, or to love as Jesus
>   loved, can't be generated purely from within.
>
> Grace is what you need. And if you are best friends with Jesus, let
> him nourish you through the Eucharist, fill you and strengthen you
> during prayer, forgive you in reconciliation—grace is what you've
> got.

Lifelines

Your life means something. God gave it to you for a reason. That
reason is, in a mysterious way, connected to the possibility of your
eternal life.

So. What is it?

There are, of course, a lot of answers to that question. These
days, perhaps the most common one is that the purpose of your
life is to discover and explore "self-fulfillment."

Really, really wrong.

We could critique the gospel of self-fulfillment from a lot of
angles, but we'll just stick to the Christian critique here.

***If you claim to be a Christian . . . self-fulfillment is not the
purpose of your life.***

It's just not. Go back and skim through those Gospels we've
been alluding to and encouraging you to read. Go back and listen
to Jesus.

Is he preaching about self-fulfillment?

Not quite.

> "This is my commandment, that you love one another as I have loved
> you. Greater love has no man than this, that a man lay down his life
> for his friends. You are my friends if you do what I command you.
> No longer do I call you servants, for the servant does not know what
> his master is doing; but I have called you friends, for all that I have
> heard from my Father I have made known to you. You did not choose
> me, but I chose you and appointed you so that you should go and

> bear fruit and that your fruit should abide; so that whatever you ask the Father in my name, he may give it to you. This I command you, to love one another."
>
> Jn 15:12-17

No, if you're a Christian, you take your cues on life's purpose from no one else but Jesus. Shut everything else out, no matter how fantastic it sounds, no matter how promising, and just listen to Jesus.

The purpose of your life is to love God and serve Him.

What that means will be different in its specifics for each of us, because God's gift of life is different and unique for everyone He's loved into existence. It's not a call for all of us to enter religious life, either. One person might love and serve God most powerfully through direct service to the poor, another through running an ethically sound business that creates and brings something helpful into the world. One person might offer thanks to God for the gift of life by tending to the sick and dying, another through raising a great family.

But the thread running through all of these lives is putting God first.

Because, if you're honest about it, in the end, who else is left?

What can you take with you?

What else will there be, but you and God, with you standing there with your life, saying, "This is what I did with the gift"?

In short

It's all about discipleship.

No matter where your talents or interests take you, the bottom line is . . . can you love and serve God and His people this way? As you choose what kind of life you're going to live, are you saying "yes" to God, are you saying "no," or are you saying "it doesn't matter"?

The next few chapters are about the temptations we all face to live by "no" or "it doesn't matter," or even simply that gospel of self-fulfillment, cut off from any consideration of what Jesus actually says about life and what it's for.

This book is about "the good life," and up to this point, we've been exploring one dimension of that phrase: how living connected to Jesus through his Church opens the door to the good — as in peaceful and joyful — life.

Now we're going to flip it, and dig around the other meaning, as in "good," which is the opposite of "bad." As in a life that embodies the quality we call "goodness"; as in a life that other people look at and say, "Wow. What a good person."

And the thing is, the two meanings are really closely connected. The more we say "yes" to Jesus, the more we live as disciples of his instead of disciples to our own desires or the demands of the world, the more deeply we experience something, something we never expected to find, but, ironically, we do anyway, as just one more gift piled on another:

Fulfillment.

In other words — the clearest road to enjoying the *good life* —

— is living . . .

— *a good life.*

Try it. What have you got to lose that's worth keeping, anyway?

CHAPTER 11

It Hurts

The good life has God at its heart.

Why? Because, as we've been saying over and over, God's the source of life, God gave it to you, God knows what is going to bring you fulfillment. Listen to Him — and you're there.

No matter how much it hurts.

Is that the strangest point we've made so far? Perhaps.

But if you don't get it, you don't get the good life.

Literally.

Pain, gain, etc.

I won't be coy about this. The point of this chapter is that a huge part of discipleship is accepting the place and (mysterious) purpose of pain and suffering in life.

In fact, most of our sins — most of our many steps backward, away from God — come about because we'd rather not suffer, thanks.

(Just think about it for a minute, to see how true it is.)

It's not that a disciple of Jesus actively seeks suffering or revels in it in some weird sort of masochistic perversion of spirituality. Not at all. It's that . . . well, just listen to Jesus.

> "If any man would come after me, let him deny himself and take up his cross and follow me. For whoever would save his life will lose it, and whoever loses his life for my sake will find it. For what will it profit a man, if he gains the whole world and forfeits his life? Or what shall a man give in return for his life?"
>
> Mt 16:24-26

And more importantly, watch him.

> And when they came to the place which is called The Skull, there they crucified him, and the criminals, one on the right and one on the left. And Jesus said, "Father, forgive them; for they know not what they do."
>
> Lk 23:33-34

There's probably a part of us that recoils from this, that just doesn't want it to be so, that wishes it were different. That's okay. That's natural. As I said, while it's unhealthy to run from suffering, it's rather unhealthy to seek it out, as well.

But here's something else to consider. Why is it that we somehow think that we can live life to the fullest, as God wants, without suffering . . . when we're perfectly willing to accept a degree of suffering as a necessary element of other parts of our lives?

We've touched on them before, but it bears repeating, because suffering is one of those things we never seem to really get.

But we know, obviously, that if you want to be healthy, you have to pay a price (most of us do, that is). You can't indulge your appetites. You have to sacrifice some pleasure. If you really appreciate being in shape, you're going to be spending time exercising, and even though it can be enjoyable, a good workout can also involve pain.

If you're in, planning to attend, or have attended graduate school, you know that success in that hothouse of competition isn't easy. In fact, sometimes, it's hell.

The same goes for establishing yourself in a profession, or even just sticking it out in a job. Bosses and co-workers can be strange, irrational, and unpleasant. You watch helplessly as the under-qualified brown-nosers flatter their way up the ladder while your work goes unappreciated.

And relationships? Well, we know all about that. Self-centered jerks, unwilling to sacrifice, usually end up alone for a reason.

So yeah, we get it in terms of the parts. Sacrifice, pain, deferred gratification = good.

Now, why in the world would it be any different for life as a whole?

It's not.

As a disciple, as a person connected to God through Christ, you've chosen a path that makes a great deal of sense: accepting God's role in your life (the end *and* the beginning), you know that the only sensible, reasonable way to live is in response to Him. He made you for a reason, and He's never silent about what that is.

Your purpose in life isn't some changing, emotionally rooted "self-fulfillment." It's the truly good life for which God created you.

But because that life is lived in the world, a world in which sin still has a great deal of power . . .

Suffering happens.

And then, amazingly, life happens, too.

No way around it

Over the centuries, Christians have come up with a lot of ways to talk about suffering. All of them try to walk that tricky road of balancing God's power, God's goodness, and our free will. We could write volumes on the subject, but we won't, because lots of other people already have.

But just remember this:

For some reason, suffering is a part of life. God doesn't "want" us to suffer. He takes no pleasure in it. He doesn't design your life as an obstacle course, chuckling as you stumble and fall.

After all, think back to Genesis. Think back to what those first couple of chapters tell us about God's intentions for His creation — which includes your life. Suffering? Part of the plan? No.

But, because of sin, suffering is certainly a part of the result.

You can argue with it all you want, but there it is. We don't live in Eden anymore, and the more we try to pretend that we do, the more we try to pretend as if suffering is something we can avoid, ironically . . . the more we suffer.

The good news — and there is good news, of course — is that God is more powerful than even the deepest suffering. God can use absolutely anything to bring about good. The story in the Old Testament that reveals this the most clearly is, in case you haven't guessed, the story of Joseph.

No need for a detailed recap, I assume. You know about Joseph — second-to-the-youngest and very beloved son of Jacob (son of Isaac, son of Abraham, by the way). Object of his brothers' deep envy, an envy so deep that they sold him off to some traders and took his beautiful coat, red with goat's blood, back to a shocked, grieving father.

Years later, of course, things have turned. Despite some hardship along the way, Joseph's situation has improved. He's a high official in the Egyptian court, and, most importantly, is in a place where his most mysterious God-given gift — the ability to interpret dreams — has saved the lives of tens of thousands who would have otherwise died in a famine.

At the end, Joseph's brothers appear before him, afraid of any revenge he might hand out to them. After all, that was the way of the world back then. But revenge isn't on Joseph's mind. Instead, this is what he says:

"Fear not, for am I in the place of God? As for you, you meant evil against me; but God meant it for good, to bring it about that

many people should be kept alive, as they are today. So do not fear; I will provide for you and your little ones." (Gn 50:19-21)

It's a story we see repeated over and over in Scriptures and in the lives of the saints: accepting suffering doesn't mean being a masochist. It doesn't mean celebrating suffering and pain. It means this:

A faith that even in this, God can — and will — work.

The story reaches its climax in the other part of the Bible — the New Testament.

After all, what else is the story of Jesus, but a story of suffering accepted for the greatest reason of all: love?

What we face

Jesus isn't silent about suffering. The Gospels are filled with his words about pain, not to speak of his own encounters with it. Since we're disciples, we can expect to face what he did:

❋ We'll suffer because we're trying to live in love. We don't want to harm others, but in the process might get harmed. (Mt 5:1-12)

❋ We'll suffer because the world is frankly hostile to Jesus. (Mt 10:16-3)

❋ We'll suffer because we join others in their own pain, out of love, instead of running away. (Jn 11:35)

❋ We'll suffer because our families and friends won't get it. (Mt 10:37-39)

❋ We'll suffer because we'll confront our own sinfulness. (Mt 26:69-74)

❋ We'll suffer because no matter how hard it works at tricking us, there's still evil, it still wants to claim us, and it will go any length to do so, or at the very least, shut us up. (Mt 26-27)

Finally, when you're committed to letting God's voice be the one that guides your decisions, it will hurt to say goodbye to other voices, other hopes, and other dreams. It will hurt to say goodbye to the dream that you can just use someone for pleasure, drop them and still be a "good person." It will hurt to say goodbye to the good feelings that stuff can give us, for a while. It also hurts pretty badly to allow yourself to be known for the person you really are, instead of for a fantasy you'd like to have the world believe.

But what are you going to do?

What's the alternative?

It's a rather important, basic question.

You're a free person. You can choose to run the other way, to live a life in which your primary goal is to avoid a little pain here, or more pain there.

Go ahead. See ya.

What happens then?

Is the suffering gone yet? Is life a giddy round of unending pleasure?

No. All you've done is shift the weight of it a little bit—for a while, at least. You've put the suffering on other people's shoulders —the people you're using, the people you're hurting. You're hiding because it hurts too much to tell the truth. You're indulging because it hurts too much to say "no." You're building up a thick wall behind which you're hiding, and quite well, thanks.

Hiding usually happens to people who are alone, though. Did you ever notice that?

The point is this:

Suffering and pain happen. To all of us. Some of it is avoidable. Some of it's not. Some suffering is unnecessary, but some . . . just happens. It happens because growth, confrontation with the truth and sticking with the good hurts. Why does it hurt?

Frankly, because there really is a darkness out there that does *not* want truth to spread, that does *not* want love to flourish, that does *not* want you to understand how deeply God loves you just as you are, and would much rather you waste your life running, hurting, and pretending.

Such a mystery, this suffering business.

What's not a mystery, though, is that for the Christian, suffering has to be confronted, has to be dealt with, and is very often a part of discipleship.

If this is just too puzzling for you, walk into any Catholic church and look up above the altar. What do you see?

Suffering, yes. But what else?

Could it be — love?

Could it be that the suffering and the love are somehow, some way intertwined, and to try to separate them is not only foolish, but leads to emptiness?

Yes, suffering is a part of a disciple's life, and its presence demands a question. Just be careful that you ask the right one. Be careful that you're not asking, "Will this choice help me avoid suffering?" but rather:

"Will this choice bring me closer to the good life that God calls me to — no matter if I suffer on the way or not?"

Ask the right questions.

No way you're going to get the right answers without them.

CHAPTER 12

Bodies and Souls

The thing is, you're both.

Body and soul, that is.

You're not a soul imprisoned in a worthless body, and you're not just a mass of tissue with no spiritual dimension, either.

Mysteriously, fantastically, oddly enough . . . you're both.

Now . . . and forever, too.

This is the real you. Get used to it.

In the beginning

We can sit around and philosophize all day about what God could have and should have done with his creatures. But no matter what we imagine . . . here we still are, doing the imagining, creatures of flesh and spirit inextricably intertwined, constructed that way by God:

The L**ord** God formed man of dust from the ground, and breathed into his nostrils the breath of life; and man became a living being. (Gn 2:7)

So what?

Here's what:

God made us as embodied, enfleshed creatures. That means that these bodies... matter. It means, first of all, like the rest of creation, these bodies are good, as God declares over and over in Genesis.

It also means that what you do with your body can't be separated from your life.

If the good life is our goal, if we've accepted the reality that God is the source of the good life here and now, that means that our choices about what to do with these bodies are just like the rest of our choices:

They bring us closer to the good life that God wants us to have...

Or they take us further away.

This is news?

Obvious, right?

Well, perhaps. But maybe not so obvious. You might want to think about the stuff you will your body to do, all the while convincing yourself that this particular act or habit has absolutely no impact on your relationship with God, that you can still be a "good Catholic" or "close to God" while you're using your body (and maybe someone else's) in ways that remind no one of the good.

> O LORD, thou hast searched me and known me!
>
> Thou knowest when I sit down and when I rise up; thou discernest my thoughts from afar.
>
> Thou searchest out my path and my lying down, and art acquainted with all my ways.
>
> Even before a word is on my tongue, lo, O LORD, thou knowest it altogether.
>
> For thou didst form my inward parts, thou didst knit me together in my mother's womb.
>
> I praise thee, for thou art fearful and wonderful. Wonderful are thy works! Thou knowest me right well;

> my frame was not hidden from thee, when I was being made in secret, intricately wrought in the depths of the earth.
>
> Thy eyes beheld my unformed substance; in thy book were written, every one of them, the days that were formed for me, when as yet there was none of them.
>
> How precious to me are thy thoughts, O God! How vast is the sum of them!
>
> If I would count them, they are more than the sand. When I awake, I am still with thee.
>
> Ps 139:1-4, 13-18

Oh, really?

This isn't about rules or that little, powerful, very loud word, "NO." Sure, you may have been accustomed to thinking about these issues in those terms, but once again, I'm daring you to stop doing so and focus on two simple points:

First, I promise you that the traditional, fairly universal understanding of the best, most moral ways to treat our bodies and the bodies of others was not dreamed up by a committee convened to make your life less pleasurable. They're rooted in experience and wisdom. Centuries of it.

Second, there's our focus:

Our focus is Jesus.

We've decided that the good life, the one that takes Jesus' hand and is led out of the tombs, is one that continues on the road of discipleship with him.

Jesus had a body. What did he do with it? How did he treat it? **Come, follow me.**

Temples

We're not talking slavish, moment-by-moment imitation here, since we are following various paths that are different from Jesus' in their specifics: we work in offices, we marry, we live in a different culture completely. We're talking about a more general pattern of life — *the good life* — that Jesus models for us; that Jesus, through His Word and His Church, enables us to live as well.

The answer is pretty simple:

With his body, just like the rest of his being, Jesus served God and others.

There.

You want more? Okay ...

As the Son of God made flesh, Jesus embraced other people in love and friendship. He ate with them, drank with them, laughed, partied, and worked.

He used his fingers and hands to heal, to indicate love and forgiveness, to comfort.

He used his feet to walk to those who needed God's love.

And finally, he gave over himself — body and spirit — to the Father, for us, out of the deepest, most passionate, committed love ever seen.

He held nothing back, body and soul, when real love was at stake.

Come, follow me ...

Hundreds of years of reflection and observation have produced a lot of wisdom in the Christian tradition, wisdom that we're foolish to ignore.

One of the most enduring points of wisdom is the understanding that there are a few attitudes that are really basic to the good life. Nurture them, and you're on the way. They're called virtues:

* Prudence: figure out the good and choose it. (Prov 14:15)
* Justice: give God and your neighbor what they deserve. (Lev 19:15)
* Fortitude: stay strong as you try to do good. (Jn 16:33)
* Temperance: keep everything in its place in your life. (Tit 2:12)
* Faith: believe God is and what God says is true. (Jn 12:44-46)
* Hope: trust that God wants the best for us. (Heb 6:19-20)
* Charity: love God and our neighbor, no matter what. (Jn 15:9-10)

No rules, just right

And that is the bottom line, that's the question we need to ask our-selves every time we're faced with a choice about our bodies — and I'm not just talking about sex either, in case you were wondering.

Take it anyplace, anytime. It's handy, and to the point.

I'm drinking my tail off or getting high every weekend, killing many brain cells, laying waste to the already short time I've got on earth, making big chunks of it nothing more than a blur.

This is why God gave me a body? For this?

I'm giving in to every — or at least most — sexual temptation that I encounter, with others or even just myself with the kind assistance of the lovely folks cavorting on my computer screen.

This is the best I can do? This is entertaining and pleasurable for a while, sure, but what's the point? Sorry, but . . . do I really think this is why God gave me the ability to experience these sen-sations? To take me deeper into myself? Or could there possibly be a bigger reason, connected to . . . God?

I'm plopping down on my couch at 7 PM and watching TV or playing video games until 11, at which point I sit down in another spot in my apartment and chat mindlessly with strangers or surf for porn or shop or do some gaming on the internet for another hour or two.

Nice connecting there. Good growth, great immersion in life in all of its mystery and possibility, fantastic attending to those in need.

Just what your body was created for.

Not.

Am I serving God with my body when I do this?

Is this bringing me closer to God?

Is this really going to bring me deeper into the good life?

What is this act about? Is it about the fantastic hopes God has for me, the potential I have to help make the world a better place, deep-

> ening real love . . . or is it about me, my senses, my needs and my
> fears?
>
> Which is it?

Short, but sweet

If you want to delve more deeply into the specifics, there are plenty of good resources written just for that purpose. I've got some listed at the back of the book.

But my purpose in this short chapter isn't to be comprehensive and detailed; it's been simply to help you see the big picture — the biggest of all. To just accept the reality that if you've decided to live for Jesus . . . you've decided to live for Jesus.

Body and soul.

A phrase which includes, you might notice — body.

Sometimes we try to get around the painful, sacrificial elements of this part of discipleship by declaring that it's all about "love" because that's what Jesus was about, and as long as we're feeling "love" or even (gag) "fulfillment" while we're using our bodies, then we're in great shape.

You should see by now how wrong that is. Why? Because we can very easily define "love" in any way we please. And the hard truth is, left to our own devices, left to the very strong temptations of pleasure, we will go ahead and do just that — we'll define it in amazingly creative, usually deeply self-serving ways. Looking back, you can probably admit to times you've done just this. You might even remember times you've been batted around, all in the name of "love."

But we're Christians. So that means, our definition of love is Jesus! Period.

And what is love?

God is love, of course.

So when Jesus' disciples make decisions about what to do with their bodies and how, love — *as God defines it* — is what we base those decisions on.

And what is that God-centered love?

Simple:

Since it's God-centered, it means seeing yourself and others through God's eyes, which are, by definition, the eyes of love. Wanting for yourself what God wants. Wanting for others what God wants.

And acting like it. With your body — every part.

If you think about it honestly, and consider those bad old "traditional" moral stances that the Church stubbornly maintains, you'll see the wisdom, and you might even see the love. You'll see, perhaps even from your own experience, that using another person's body for pleasure ended up in nothing but hurt, and might have even blinded you to that other person's true beauty and worth. You might see the waste and suffering that comes from misuse of alcohol and drugs and find yourself wondering what might have been, if only the person indulging — you or someone you love — had just tried a little harder to cling to God and have the guts to experience life as it is, rather than retreating behind a haze. You might see that there is something amazingly freeing about going to bed only with the one you've vowed your life to; someone you've vowed to serve and help toward holiness, someone with whom you're open to raising a family — no matter when God sends those kids, because those kids are nothing but walking, talking, breathing signs of love — someone whom you know will be there and love you tomorrow, next week, and twenty years down the line.

Just as Christian tradition has discerned virtues fundamental to the good life, it's also discerned vices or sins that are destructive to the good life. They're called "capital" or, more commonly, the "Seven Deadly Sins":

* Pride: I don't need anyone, even God. (Gn 3:1-5)

* Greed: I want stuff, no matter what the price. (Ex 20:17)

* Envy: I'm not happy with who I am. (Gn 4:3-7)

* Anger: I wish ill for you. (Mt 5:22)

* Lust: I'll use you for my own pleasure. (Mt 5:27-28)

* Gluttony: I want, and I don't care if others don't have. (Prov 28:7)

* Sloth: I don't care. Let life pass me by. (Mt 26:41)

You might be seeing that when it comes to bodies, there's a love and joy God built into this whole system — that's the place of light and real freedom, of service and sacrifice, and that's a much better place than the alternative: the place of fear, secrets, mistrust, and hearts and lives closed to life.

It's not just better.

It's good. It's a really *good* life.

In every way.

If I speak in the tongues of men and of angels, but have not love, I am a noisy gong or a clanging cymbal.

And if I have prophetic powers, and understand all mysteries and all knowledge, and if I have all faith, so as to remove mountains, but have not love, I am nothing. If I give away all I have, and if I deliver my body to be burned, but have not love, I gain nothing.

Love is patient and kind; love is not jealous or boastful; it is not arrogant or rude.

Love does not insist on its own way; it is not irritable or resentful; it does not rejoice at wrong, but rejoices in the right.

Love bears all things, believes all things, hopes all things, endures all things.

Love never ends . . .

So faith, hope, love abide, these three; but the greatest of these is love.

1 Cor 13

CHAPTER 13

Lifetime

By now, The Good Life should be fairly clear:

You, hooked into Jesus, through His Body, the Church, listening, loving, serving.

But there really is one more thing, a missing piece from this picture we're painting:

The life part. Like — where you go after your alarm rings, you're out of the shower and dressed for success. Who signs your paycheck. What you *do* with the paycheck. Where your energy is going, what your talents are being used for, and what, when it's all just about done, you're going to look back at and say, "Well. That wasn't a waste."

Twenty-four hours per day. Seven days per week, four weeks per month. Maybe 600 months on earth ahead of you, more or less.

Why?

What's wrong

I used to teach high school, and the question of goals was one that came up regularly. What do you want out of life, I'd ask. The answers were almost always a variation of this:

"A job doing something I love, making me enough money to be comfortable. And travel — I want to travel."

Everyone always wanted to travel.

Nice goals. Not too greedy, sort of realistic.

And thoroughly, totally secular. Even the pagans, Jesus might say, would wish as much for themselves.

That might be something to think about. What good is any of the rest of the stuff we've been talking about in this book if your basic goals in life, your sense of what your time on earth is all about, *is no different from those of someone who* doesn't *put God at the center of his or her life?*

Then all of this other stuff is nothing but window-dressing, is the answer. It's just one more self-help scheme, one more road to feeling good about ourselves, instead of a really radical reorientation of our life toward The One who gave it to us in the first place, and (don't forget) The One whom we are going to face after it's all done.

So we're just going to be brutally frank about this:

Personal professional success isn't an adequate life goal for a disciple.

Material comfort, much less wealth, doesn't capture it either.

Getting stuff, building wealth, early retirement . . . and yeah, even travel.

We can do better.

In fact, we *have to.*

Or else it really is all just a game, and our "faith" is something we use to increase our sense of security or well-being, instead of being the essence of who we are.

Do you not believe me? Are you mad yet?

Well, go back, then. Ponder again those Gospels we've been reading and pondering throughout this book.

And answer this—

What does Jesus say your life is for?

If you belong to him . . . that's your answer, too.

> "You are the light of the world. A city set on a hill cannot be hid. Nor do men light a lamp and put it under a bushel, but on a stand, and it gives light to all in the house. Let your light so shine before men, that they may see your good works and give glory to your Father who is in heaven."
>
> Mt 5:14-16

What it means . . . and doesn't

The world tells you that the good life lies in professional success, a certain degree of what it calls "excellence" and material comfort, or even prosperity.

And travel. Can't forget the travel.

Good for them. But it's not the good life that God—who knows a little bit about it—shows us.

No, the good life for the disciple lies in something radical, something simple, and something profound:

Waking up each morning and praying, *God, thank you for this life. It's unique and amazing. What do you want me to do with it today? How can I serve?*

Do you see the difference?

And, most importantly, do you see how wildly different the fruit of this life is going to be?

For the reality is, if your goal when you wake up every morning is to be materially successful, to climb the ladder, to make more money, or even to fulfill your marvelous, fantastic potential, there's a good chance that you will spend a great deal of your life being incredibly frustrated.

Why? Because you'll live your days, weeks and those 600 months (more or less) as a hostage to two things: the world, and your own desires. You'll be making your decisions based on how others will respond to you and what they'll give you. You'll be choosing a path that will get you stuff, only to see the stuff rot, go out of fashion, or just whet your thirst for more stuff.

In other words — *you won't be free.*

But with God, even though we're talking about serving God as the center of our life, this weird thing happens: When you wake up each morning trusting that God loves you, that He gave you this life to make something good out of, and that in the end, *you're only accountable to Him...*

You're free.

Free to be yourself, free from the negative impact of others' judgments, free from the prison of desire.

Just free.

What it doesn't mean

Don't get the wrong idea. This isn't a clarion call for every one of us to enter religious life. That's never been what this is all about, even from the earliest days of Christianity. Paul kept making tents, even after his conversion and commitment to living for Christ.

You have tents to make as well.

The point isn't *what* you do (mostly — there are certain professions that would most definitely be Not On The List. You can probably figure out what those might be) —but *why* you do it and *how.*

Your talents and choices may still lead you into corporate law or television production, nursing, teaching, plumbing, or ... anything. You may very well give years of your life to medical or business school, working hard, giving huge chunks of your brain over to all the information you need in order to follow that career.

But, again ... *why?*

If we're following Jesus, we can still follow any of those career paths and do most of what they require. This world is a diverse, rich place. Part of what we do as human beings is to build on God's original vision, using the gifts He gave us for that purpose. We create, we invent, we entertain, we make life easier for others, we reduce unnecessary suffering, we work with God in countless ways, walking down countless paths. Everyone — the sanitation worker, the electronic engineer, the visual artist, the therapist, the priest, the nursing home aide, the parent rocking a baby . . . everyone plays a part.

But that is the crucial phrase, and the one that makes all the difference: we're playing a *part* in God's creation, pulling our own little thread of talent in this vast tapestry, and doing *it in service to God and others.*

Not to get rich. *Not* to be successful. *Not* to travel.

But . . . to *serve.*

Stuff

One of the reasons we all have jobs is because we want money to buy stuff.

And to travel.

Some of the stuff, we need, a lot of it we don't.

What's a disciple to do?

Well, the answer to that should be fairly clear right now — follow Jesus (that's what Christian disciples do). Listen. Live.

> A scribe came up and said to him, "Teacher, I will follow you wherever you go." And Jesus said to him, "Foxes have holes, and birds of the air have nests; but the Son of man has nowhere to lay his head." Another of the disciples said to him, "Lord, let me first go and bury my father." But Jesus said to him, "Follow me, and leave the dead to bury their own dead."
>
> Mt 8:19-22

> "Do not lay up for yourselves treasures on earth, where moth and rust consume and where thieves break in and steal . . . No one can serve two masters; for either he will hate the one and love the other, or he will be devoted to the one and despise the other. You cannot serve God and mammon."
>
> Mt 6: 19-20, 24

And he lifted up his eyes on his disciples, and said:

"Blessed are you poor, for yours is the kingdom of God.

"Blessed are you that hunger now, for you shall be satisfied.

"Blessed are you that weep now, for you shall laugh.

"Blessed are you when men hate you, and when they exclude you
      and revile you, and cast out your name as evil, on account
      of the Son of man!

Rejoice in that day, and leap for joy, for behold, your reward is
      great in heaven; for so their fathers did to the prophets.

"But woe to you that are rich,
      for you have received your consolation.

"Woe to you that are full now, for you shall hunger.

"Woe to you that laugh now, for you shall mourn and weep.

"Woe to you, when all men speak well of you, for so their fathers
      did to the false prophets."

Lk 6:20-26

Through much of our history, Christians have spent a lot of time downplaying these words. We gloss over them; we redefine them; we declare that Jesus didn't really mean them.

In short, we stand in judgment of Jesus rather than getting on our knees and letting him stand in judgment of us. We define him, instead of opening ourselves to the truth we claim we believe in and letting it define us.

Some disciples.

Jesus' teaching on wealth is admittedly difficult to take. But it might be useful to admit that even as we regularly blow it off, we also do, deep down, admit its truth. How? By holding up figures like St. Francis of Assisi and Blessed Mother Teresa, disciples who have really lived the Gospel. We honor them, we admire them, we shake our heads and declare how glad we are that someone, some-where, is taking Jesus seriously here.

But why not us?

Look, it's the constant struggle of many of us, particularly in a wealthy society. The temptation of stuff is so strong, for countless reasons: Stuff is, well ... cool. It's fun. It feels good. Looks good. Rides really good. On a deeper level, we use stuff to prove something about ourselves to the world. We surround ourselves with it so that the world won't mistake us for losers.

So what is Jesus saying about stuff, anyway? If I'm committed to following Jesus — if I understand whatever it is I'm doing to earn my money as a service — and I'm still making money (it happens) and have the ability to buy stuff ... what then? Is the stuff inherently evil?

No, that's not what Jesus is saying at all. He's saying, very simply, that material wealth *gets in the way* of our relationship with God. Invariably.

It doesn't help. In fact, *it can hurt.*

How? Several ways. We can get distracted by the pursuit of the stuff, and neglect God — that is, we can work for twelve hours a day, and then declare our time is too precious, or we're just too tired, to take fifteen minutes of it to pray.

We can trick ourselves into thinking that the pleasure we get out of a great car, computer, or whatever it is that floats our boat ... completes us. To put it bluntly, that because of the stuff, we don't need God.

So we turn away.

And we find ourselves, at some point, in a place in which the stuff not only can't help us, it seems to mock us: "See," it says, "you spent all of your energy going after us, and now here you are, with a broken relationship, an illness, a death ... but so sorry. We can't help."

And finally, there is the whole justice issue — not an extra point to consider for disciples of Jesus, but really at the core of who we are. It is perhaps not the greatest evil in the world to spend two hundred times the yearly income of a family in the Dominican Republic on a car for yourself, but . . .

It's not the height of holiness, either.

And to be brutally frank about it, it's hard to see how a serious disciple of Jesus, one who is intent on letting Jesus be your best friend and guide, can fit in self-indulgent spending habits with that friendship.

There are people in great need in the world. These people are not "other." They are our brothers and sisters. They are the face of Jesus. We have a relationship to them. Our decisions about stuff can't be made in a vacuum.

Hard. Kind of frustrating. But true.

It's nice to admire what Jesus says or St. Francis' stance towards wealth. But amid all the admiration, we have to be honest: a disciple isn't called just to admire Jesus' words, be glad he said them, and declare that yeah, the world would be a better place if everyone agreed with Jesus.

Disciples don't just nod in agreement.

Disciples follow. Disciples live.

"Not every one who says to me, 'Lord, Lord,' shall enter the kingdom of heaven, but he who does the will of my Father who is in heaven." (Mt 7:21)

Real life

This is all rooted, of course, in the Gospels.

But if you've ever known a middle-aged person, you know that there's some very basic human truth that even pagans can see as well.

After all, what is the famed "mid-life crisis" all about?

It's about wondering . . . *what have I been doing for the past twenty years? What good did I do? Was it just a waste?*

When you're out to serve yourself, and not much else, when you've lived your life under the judgment of others... that's exactly what happens.

So what does this mean in terms of the basic realities of your life? Well, that's something only you can figure out—with God's help, and maybe with the help of good spiritual director, too. A fellow disciple of Jesus who's on the same wavelength can help you pick through your God-given talents, the moments that life is holding out to you, and the call of Jesus—and figure out where to go next.

It also means that you're slowly but surely going to push your own ego out of the center of consideration. Strange, but true. The more you listen to Jesus, the more you're going to understand that, just as he said and lived, true joy—now and forever—comes from putting yourself aside and putting God, and love of others, at the center of your decisions.

It's as simple as this:

Jesus shows us the way. He lived completely for others.

His way—our way.

Period.

It also means that change is going to happen, and it's time to be open to that. Sometimes we might think of great saints as people who stick to one path and never get off it. Well, if the "path" you're talking about is listening to God, you're right. But if that "path" is about specific activity in the world—you're wrong.

The lives of saints are marked, at every turn, by an amazing flexibility. There's no such thing as a saint in a rut. Saints like Frances Cabrini and Francis Xavier traveled literally all over the world, depending on where they felt God was calling them. Saints like St. Vincent de Paul and Elizabeth Ann Seton were forever starting new projects, trying to figure out new ways to bring God's love into this amazingly diverse world.

No ruts. No imprisonment to the world's judgment. No unquenchable desire for stuff that rots anyway. An overflowing love for all of God's creation and each of God's children. The freedom to live it and share the love of Christ, and end our lives on earth, not in fear or disappointment, but in gratitude and hope, knowing we have said — and lived — "yes."

A life that may have gotten lost amid the tombs for a while, but now, drawn out by the loving hand of Jesus, saved. Alive. Grateful. Free.

Sounds great to me.

Sounds a little bit like . . . the good life.

Further Reading

Augustine, St. *Confessions.*

Bonacci, Mary Beth. *Real Love: Answers to Your Questions on Dating, Marriage and the Real Meaning of Sex.* Ignatius, 1996.

Catechism of the Catholic Church. Our Sunday Visitor, 2000.

Day, Dorothy. *The Long Loneliness.* HarperSanFrancisco, 1997.

De Sales, Francis. *Introduction to the Devout Life.* Image, 1972.

Dubruiel, Michael. *How To Get the Most From the Eucharist.* Our Sunday Visitor, 2005.

_____. *The How-To Book of the Mass.* Our Sunday Visitor, 2002.

_____. *The Power of the Cross: Applying the Passion of Christ to Your Life.* Our Sunday Visitor, 2004.

Groeschel, Benedict. *Listening at Prayer.* Paulist Press, 1984.

_____. *Spiritual Passages: The Psychology of Spiritual Development "for Those Who Seek."* Crossroad Publishing Company, 1984.

Johnson, Luke Timothy. *The Creed.* Image, 2004.

Kavanaugh, John F. *Following Christ in a Consumer Society: The Spirituality of Cultural Resistance.* Orbis Books, 1991.

Kreeft, Peter. *Catholic Christianity: A Complete Catechism of Catholic Beliefs Based on the Catechism of the Catholic Church.* Ignatius Press, 2001.

Kurey, Mary-Louise. *Standing with Courage: Confronting Tough Decisions about Sex.* Our Sunday Visitor, 2002.

Lickona, Matthew. *Swimming with Scapulars.* Loyola, 2005.

Merton, Thomas. *Seven Storey Mountain.* Harcourt, 1999.

O'Conner, Flannery. *The Habit of Being.* Farrar, Straus and Giroux, 1988.

Welborn, Amy. *Prove It! Church.* Our Sunday Visitor, 2001.

_____. *Prove It! God.* Our Sunday Visitor, 2000.

_____. *Prove It! Jesus.* Our Sunday Visitor, 2002.

_____. *Prove It! Prayer.* Our Sunday Visitor, 2002.

_____. *Prove It! The Catholic Teen Bible.* Our Sunday Visitor, 2004.

_____. *The Words We Pray.* Loyola, 2004.

West, Christopher. *Good News About Sex and Marriage: Answers to Your Honest Questions About Catholic Teaching.* Servant Books, 2000.

Stories for the Good Life

Connelly, Myles. *Mr. Blue*. Loyola Press, 2005.

Endo, Shusaky. *Silence*. Parkwest, 1980.

Greene, Graham. *The Power and the Glory*. Penguin USA, 2003.

O'Conner, Flannery. *Collected Works*. Library of America, 1988.

Percy, Walker. *Love in the Ruins*. Picador, 1999.

Waugh, Evelyn. *Brideshead Revisited*. Back Bay Books, 1999.

Notes

Our Sunday Visitor ...
Your Source for Discovering the Riches of the Catholic Faith

Our Sunday Visitor has an extensive line of materials for young children, teens, and adults. Our books, Bibles, pamphlets, CD-ROMs, audios, and videos are available in bookstores worldwide.

To receive a FREE full-line catalog or for more information, call **Our Sunday Visitor** at **1-800-348-2440, ext. 3**. Or write **Our Sunday Visitor** / 200 Noll Plaza / Huntington, IN 46750.

Please send me ___ A catalog
Please send me materials on:
___ Apologetics and catechetics
___ Prayer books
___ The family
___ Reference works
___ Heritage and the saints
___ The parish

Name _____
Address _____ Apt._____
City _____ State _____ Zip_____
Telephone ( ) _____
                                                        A53BBBBP

Please send a friend ___ A catalog
Please send a friend materials on:
___ Apologetics and catechetics
___ Prayer books
___ The family
___ Reference works
___ Heritage and the saints
___ The parish

Name _____
Address _____ Apt._____
City _____ State _____ Zip_____
Telephone ( ) _____
                                                        A53BBBBP

OurSundayVisitor

200 Noll Plaza, Huntington, IN 46750
Toll free: **1-800-348-2440**
Website: www.osv.com